SACRED FIREPLACE

(OCETI WAKAN)

**Life and Teachings of a
37th Generation Lakota
Medicine Man**

With much love and devotion, I dedicate this book to *Okawinga Win* (Perpetual Cycle Woman), Amelia Emily Ribsman Catches, and all *Wakunka* (Elders) who hold the eternal female embodiment of the Great Mystery's infinity of love. It is they who teach *wakanyeja* (sacred beings, children) into adulthood. In the Spotted Eagle Clan and the Sundance Nation, *Okawinga Win's* spirit lives as a true and loving flower of a matriarch forever in bloom.

~Peter V. Catches (*Zintkala Oyate*)

SACRED FIREPLACE
(OCETI WAKAN)

Life and Teachings of a 37th Generation Lakota Medicine Man

Pete S. Catches Sr.
(Petaga Yuha Mani)

with

Peter V. Catches
(Zintkala Oyate)

Oceti Wakan, Publisher, Pine Ridge, SD

copyright: 1999 by Peter V. Catches
Oceti Wakan
P O Box 1958
Pine Ridge, SD 57770
www.ocetiwakan.org

All rights reserved. No part of this book may be reproduced in any form or by any electronic or mechanical means, including information storage and retrieval systems, without permission in writing from the publisher.

Second Edition
Library of Congress Control Number: 2011960427

Library of Congress Cataloging-in-Publication Data
Catches, Pete; Sacred Fireplace: Life and Teachings of a 37th Generation Lakota Medicine Man / Pete S. Catches Sr. with Peter V. Catches

ISBN 9780965862615
1. Catches, Pete. 2. Oglala Indians-Religion. 3. Oglala Indians-Biography 4. Shamans-South Dakota Biography. 5. Native American spirituality. 6. Lakota spirituality ceremonies
I. Catches, Peter V. II Title

Photos: copyright Peter V. Catches family collection: Forward, Preface , Pages: 1, 11, 70, 85, 94, 127, 140, 142, 146,161, 174, 178, 198, 227, 232, 233, 238. Copyright photos by David Zimmerly with permission: pages: 31, 45, 188, 192, 195, 207. Picture p. 74 with permission from NMAI. Oceti Wakan picture and drawings by Kate Chesley

Editor: Cindy Catches and Barbara Kohl
Book Interior Design Production: Cindy Catches
Cover Design: Alice Williams and Cindy Catches
Printed by Wons Printing Company Limited
www.wonsprinting.com, Email: Yeafw@163.com

TABLE OF CONTENTS

Forward
Preface
- 2 **Introduction** by *Zintkala Oyate*
- 3 The Spotted Eagle Way
- 4 The Blessing

- 12 **One (*Wanji*) Life Teachings and Experiences**
- 20 On Religion
- 24 The Great Spirit's Guiding Hand

- 32 **Two (*Nunpa*) On Being a Medicine Man**
- 32 Becoming a Medicine Man
- 45 Constitution of a Medicine Man
- 54 A Doctoring Trip to Hawaii
- 63 Praying at Difficult Times

- 70 **Three (*Yamni*) Stories and Lessons**
- 70 Lakota Creation Story - "We are Little Brother to the Buffalo"
- 74 Winter Count
- 79 The Deity of the Brave by *Zintkala Oyate*
- 85 The Legend of Pte Woku by *Zintkala Oyate*
- 94 Truth and Honesty
- 103 The Story of Blah Blah by *Zintkala Oyate*
- 107 Wounded Knee - 1973
- 127 Trip to Atlanta - 1990
- 129 Message to Chemawa Indian Students
- 134 Dr. King's Ecumenical Services

- 136 **Four (*Topa*) Ceremonies**
- 136 Radiantly I Come by *Zintkala Oyate*
- 140 Seven Sacred Rites

142 *Inipi* (Purification Rite) The First Form of Prayer
146 Preparations for *Inipi*
148 Inside the *Inipi*
151 Good Lance's Teachings
154 A Way of Life
156 Talking to the Holy Stones by *Zintkala Oyate*
161 *Hanbleceya* (Pipefast)
174 Within the Unseen Realm by *Zintkala Oyate*
178 *Wiwangyang Wacipi* (Sundance)
192 The Lone Dancer by *Zintkala Oyate*
198 *Hunkapi* (Making of a Relative)

207 **Five (Zaptan) Endings & Beginnings**
207 Land of the Winds by *Zintkala Oyate*
217 Memorial to Amelia & Pete Catches, *Oceti Wakan*
218 The Greatest Evil of Our Time
227 Purpose of Oceti Wakan

233 **Epilogue** by *Zintkala Oyate*

239 **Glossary**

We would like to take this opportunity to express our appreciation to the following people: Priscilla Magouirk for getting the Publishing Rights returned to us, which made this book possible; to David Zimmerly for the photos of Petaga Yuha Mani, taken in 1968 that he so generously shared with us. They helped us all experience this holy man to a greater degree; and to all of our friends, Alice Williams, Therese Leclair, Cathlee Mozinski, and Debby Howe who spent their valuable time proof reading.

FOREWORD

by *Zintkala Oyate*

The words in this book are from Lakotas speaking in an oral tradition. The type of editing undertaken retains the spirit and energy of the language, which embody and derive from the natural philosophy inherent in the culture of the Lakota *Oyate*. Previous books about the Lakota people have been devoid of the quality in which these people interact, thereby distorting the full meaning of their language and mindset. Something is lost when English syntax is formed around written translations of the Lakota as well as the words spoken by a person who thinks in Lakota. What we have attempted here is to keep the interpretation as authentic as possible.

PREFACE

by *Zintkala Oyate*

When I was a young boy, we lived at a place called Calico, a village between three and four miles northwest of the town of Pine Ridge, South Dakota, on Highway 18. The Calico Meeting Hall is now a large, dilapidated, one-room log house, with two chimneys on each side and three tall cottonwood trees in front. The White Clay Creek flows on the same side of the highway as the meeting hall. Evidence of change lies to the north, where in the foothills, covered with beautiful pine trees, is a church near a white cliff known as White Bank.

The story goes that one Easter a boy relative gave me a gift of a raccoon. I guess they didn't let the boy keep it because the raccoon got into everything. As soon as this relative told me the raccoon was mine, I fell completely in love with it. Some of you are familiar with the mannerisms of these beautiful, furry little creatures. They are a wonder to watch, particularly for little children. When you give raccoons something, they tend to wash it with their humanlike hands, or so it seems- it's a habit that makes an amusing sight. So, there I was in the middle of the floor in our house gleefully playing with my new pet, oblivious to my surroundings.

Later that evening, my mother told me to put my still unnamed pet outside. Although I begged for the raccoon to stay inside, my pleas fell on deaf ears.

The raccoon had to sleep outside. The door to our house faced south, and eight yards from the door was a shade. A type of shelter, the shade was a square, ribbed structure with pine boughs on the top and sides, and was used only in the summer. That night I tied my lovable little pet to the shade. I put out a little blanket and a bowl of water with some bread and gave the raccoon a few last pets with a loving goodnight.

The next morning my happiness was obliterated. My pet raccoon had committed suicide! The other kids mocked. Nothing of this magnitude had ever happened in my young life. I was devastated and I didn't know what to do. Somehow, I found the courage to loosen the tiny rope that held my pet suspended in mid air. I took that little blanket and wrapped his frail little body. My grandfather, who was alive at the time, told me that I must bury my pet, but in the back of my mind, I had a better idea. I said I would wait for my father. When my father came home late that afternoon, I marched right up to him with my wrapped-up raccoon and laid it at his feet. With tears in my eyes, barely able to speak, I demanded that he bring my pet raccoon back to life.

My father's gentle voice explained the matters of life and the inevitable end of everything that lived. Right then and there as a child, I accepted death as a part of our journey back to our home, the place of the Great Spirit. Often, with the death of those closest to me, with the sadness and the tears that burn cold on my cheeks, I know that death is a corridor to eternal life.

I would like to take this opportunity to thank all the people who have so generously contributed to bringing this book to publication. May the Great

Mystery bless each of you for your efforts. I want to especially acknowledge and thank my friend and nephew, Robert Holden, for the many hours he spent taping and transcribing the words of my father, *Petaga Yuha Mani*.

Pete S. Catches Sr. and grandson, Robert Holden - 1990

Zintkala Oyate

SACRED FIREPLACE

John Fire Lame Deer and Pete S. Catches Sr. in 1970 at Green Grass Sundance

INTRODUCTION

by *Zintkala Oyate*

Petaga Yuha Mani, known as Pete S. Catches, Sr., was considered a holy man of the Dakota Nation. As a 37th generation medicine man of the Spotted Eagle Clan, he taught the fundamental aspects of teachings, understandings, and ceremonies of *Canku Lute*, the Red Road of Life, or the Pipe religion, as it is known by the Lakota people. This book can help guide the reader who has an open heart.

Pete Catches Sr. was most well known for bringing the *Wiwangyang wacipi* (Sundance) into the open in the early 1960s. The Sundance and certain other Lakota rituals were driven underground in the late 1800s. Native American religion was against the law in the United States until 1979. For many years, people found practicing these rituals were subject to a ten year prison sentence and/or a $10,000 fine.

Pete Catches' commitment to returning the Sundance to the lives of the Lakota was a courageous act that gained much love and appreciation from the minds, hearts, and spirits of the Lakota people. During this time he refused many offers by people who wished to collaborate with him to write a book about his life and work, because he felt that the time was not right. Now, in these pages of 'Sacred Fireplace,' you will find glimpses of the devastation of an ancient culture, the deep-rooted sorrow of reservation life, and the rebirth of the Lakota *Oyate*. Pete Catches had a dream, or spiritual vision, of a healing center for all people, called *Oceti Wakan* (Sacred Fireplace.)

The Spotted Eagle's Way

Petaga Yuha Mani's (He Who Walks With Hot Coals) way of medicine is called the Spotted Eagle's Way. I too follow that way of doctoring. Although similar in nature, my ability in the way was by birthright and developed differently from that of my father. At my father's request, I wrote the following characterization of the Eagle's Way.

Lakota people belong to different clans, such as the Bear Clan, the Elk Clan, and the *Heyoka* Clan (people who literally do things backward in a humorous manner and whose spirit helpers are the powerful Thunder Beings). There are also ghost healers (medicine men specialized in exorcism), who do not belong to a particular clan. Each clan has its own medicine way used to help clan constituents. And each way has respective ceremonies and doctoring that are part of the clan's way of life in this world and of their conception of the spirit world.

My father and I are of the Spotted Eagle Clan. In the Eagle's Way, everything is done in the light so that everyone can see, such as the Seven Sacred Rites given to us by *Wohpe*, daughter of T*aku Skan Skan*, which include the Purification Rite, Pipefast, Sundance, healing ceremonies, to find missing loved ones, and to help people who are emotionally, mentally, spiritually, and physically ill.

INTRODUCTION

We do not hide behind covered windows or darkness.[1] Because our truths and beliefs are simple, we gain a faith that can move mountains. The Eagle's Way is the most powerful in the realms of heaven. It soars high above all others in Lakota society.

THE BLESSING

In an age long ago, there was a teacher of realms beyond. It was his nature to follow the Eagle's Way in ultimate reality of truth, and to behold Wakan Tanka's enlightenment of the absolute.

The warrior walked and came upon a gathering. He was searching for inner peace, relief from the brutality of his life. He was searching for answers to the questions that intruded upon his mind from the sadness of his cold heart. He knew of death and how his footsteps were replaced by its shadow. He knew that his loneliness kept him isolated as well as safe.

---

[1] This statement is an indirect reference to two different realities. First, because of the repression imposed on the practice of Lakota spirituality for many years, rites and ceremonies were conducted "behind covered windows" and in "darkness." Such activities went underground in order to prevent action against the Lakota involved by Bureau of Indian Affairs (BIA) representatives (as well as others who would report to the BIA). Second, medicine men of other clans use black medicine (which is also an element of life) in healing and other rites. Spotted Eagle's Way medicine men do not.

SACRED FIREPLACE

The gathering was a great coming together of spiritual teachers from many different peoples, cultures, and beliefs. Each teacher had a retinue of singers, drummers, and helpers, and each retinue wore such beautiful regalia that it was hard to distinguish which was the most magnificent. The sacred songs were done in harmonious splendor, touching the hearts of the many and causing joyous tears to flow, but the warrior remained untouched. He saw that some people were totally elated to be at this gathering, but nothing at all stirred in him.

The warrior looked beyond the magnificent display and the sonorous words and saw that none of the teachers radiated the spiritual beauty that comes from the Great Mystery. He saw that none were inspired by the eternal virtue that comes from the deity of the brave.[2] An earthly desire to be universally liked was their real ambition, and their only contribution was to please themselves. Untouched by their words, he grew angry at their falseness.

Disillusioned and disheartened, he turned away. His melancholy thoughts floundered in a sea of hopelessness where there is no love of existence. He felt powerless in a world not his own. Dimly he heard the announcer of the gathering asking for everyone's attention. "We have the final speaker," the announcer said, "a man who is the keeper of

---

[2] The "deity of the brave" refers to the sacred dream or dreams of a great Lakota warrior of the past, whose spirit lives on in the memory and recollections of the Lakota people. This term is also representative of warriors (past, present, and future) who embody the Lakota Nation's principal virtues of generosity, fortitude, fidelity, and bravery.

INTRODUCTION

the Spotted Eagle's Way." The warrior turned back to look at this last speaker and saw no entourage, no beautiful regalia. Instead, the man wore a simple ribbon shirt and a few eagle feathers in his hair. The warrior saw a man whose body and soul bore the scars of living, yet vibrated with an outpouring of energy. Feeling a strange but powerful attraction, the warrior moved closer to the center of the gathering, eager to hear the man's words. He could tell that this speaker would bless the gathering with a glimpse of the truth.

"People of the Creator," this final speaker began, "I ask you now for a moment of serene silence. In this silence pray for your love, for your life, and how you want that love to become real, for how you want to embrace life and live free, building your love slowly and feeling it grow." The warrior opened his heart to let those few words ignite a gentle understanding and felt the silence beginning.

"Fulfill the obligations that are right for you alone," the speaker continued. "They may not be many; yet be certain that you complete them in the path of your footsteps."

The warrior's mind traveled back to a long-forgotten time. He recalled clearly his childhood dream, a dream that nourished and promised a cherished tomorrow. He was filled with anguish for having betrayed his soul.

"That small inspiration begins to grow in the earth of your being," the speaker said. "It is an enlightened joy that comes from God. Knowing this, moment by moment, it becomes holy. In order to build that love, you do it day by day until, when you stand before the Great Mystery, you can say, "My God, my love, I have built my love slowly. For my love to become real, I have worked honestly so that which I have built and attained is forever, and in your love."

A tear trickled from the warrior's eye and rolled warmly down his face. The silence had truly begun. It was a blessed moment.

"Today," the speaker went on, "I stand before you, people of the Great Mystery, an advocate of the Sundance Nation, whose members are the people of peace. We all know there is a sunburst of light coming from the Creator. Each ray of light is a truth, a way of wisdom and livelihood through which each culture worships our Creator. We know God is God, and the Creator's essence is the holy swirl of this universe. Therefore, we must acknowledge and accept that we as individuals are integral to the fabric of His holy design."

The warrior felt he was at a threshold. The feelings of foreboding and anxiety that clouded his daily life were suddenly lifted and a sweet innocence took its place. He felt an awkward outpouring of change that warmed his cold heart.

"As you were told," the speaker said, "I am of the Spotted Eagle's Way, one of the clans of the Lakota people. I come here not by coincidence, but rather through a clear imprint of my footsteps in the path of my destiny. For some of you, the meaning of what I am obliged to say here will be more than you will be able to comprehend in this moment, yet the solution will remain with you until you are ready for it to flower within you. For others, it will be a profound sweetness of knowledge that you have been waiting for all of your lives, and are now eager to embrace and accept. To find and draw that hidden curtain in your mind, look behind your insipid color to find the complete sacredness of the

INTRODUCTION

one holy fire of love, and leave that door open in your heart."

The warrior did not understand these words until he glanced around the gathering. Although he saw the differences in shades of color, he closed his eyes and saw the darkness. Something wonderful happened. He heard the sounds of the people, divided by their beliefs and cultures, yet sharing an equality fed by the fire of life the Great Mystery so lovingly fashioned in their souls.

"The place where we are living now," the simple man continued, "this in-between world of worlds, this tangible reality of our known lives and the limits of our comprehension, this is what we know to be true scientifically, as our senses grasp this truth as fact. But as we stand at the alter of our quest for understanding, here below the clouds of fearful holiness, we are in the presence of the sacred gentle and loving mother of our sentient beings."

The warrior's eyes opened to a new level of consciousness, to a world that he never imagined. The cold, dark, and unloved vortex of his once lonely existence vanished. The laws and beliefs and the false greed of his ambitions lay burned to ashes by his metamorphosis, by his realization that his soul was a part of the sacred fire of the Great Mystery.

"In this whole world," the simple man said, "there is no place sacred. There is only one place sacred for you and from that place you will speak to the Great Mystery. In that place, the Great Spirit will listen to your words. It is from there that the Great Mystery has made your words holy. It is there that eternal love grows, there that the Most Holy turns to look at you . . . My time is up. I pray that the Great

SACRED FIREPLACE

Spirit's love and affection are forever yours. *Mitakuye oyasin*."

The warrior watched as this simple man, who had healed and changed his life forever, walked away through the crowd. His past was already an eternity away and forgotten. The warrior faced a bright tomorrow on an ancient but new road, the Red Road of Life.

A spiritual man of the Eagle's Way embodies the way; he has integrity, character, honor, reason, natural conduct,[3] intelligence, and wisdom. He is able to assist others in achieving unity with the Great Mystery, regardless of their situation.[4] This spiritual man is reserved. He conforms to *Wakan Tanka* and thus achieves favor with power. With power, everything is possible. A spiritual man of the Eagle's Way knows the limit and extent of his abilities in accordance with spiritual laws, as well as when to impose these laws on others.

People often do not understand this Red Road of Life because they crave intellectual knowledge. Being Lakota, following the Red Road of Life, is to live in balance and harmony. To know this ancient concept is a step toward the Eagle's Way, which is as deep and vast as the immortal. Out of *Wakan*

---

[3]"Natural conduct" in the Lakota lexicon has the connotation of carrying oneself with dignity. It includes respect of self and other people's boundaries, as well as respect for all life, or carrying oneself properly on Mother Earth.

[4]Individuals vary tremendously in terms of spiritual knowledge and attainment. A spiritual man of the Eagle's Way is capable of knowing people's individual spiritual needs, and helping them accordingly.

INTRODUCTION

Tanka comes the Eagle's Way, and from the Eagle's Way comes unity. Out of unity comes peace, healing, and harmony. When the way of the Eagle is lost, unity gives way to compassion. When compassion fades, justice without feeling or emotion prevails. And then, when justice without feeling fades, ceremonial rituals abound with the loss of self.[5]

In the Eagle's Way, foreknowledge of what will come is both good and bad. The wise person takes the good and leaves the bad, and humbly lives in the Eagle's Way. Evil is thus irrelevant - it retains power, but is unable to harm the people.

My father, *Petaga Yuha Mani*, asked me to share the Spotted Eagle Way in this simple fashion. I thank you for reading this from me, and may the Great Spirit's love and affection brighten your life and the lives of your loved ones.

---

[5] The Lakota spiritual system is based on understanding of a relationship hierarchy. At the very top is unity, wherein all life is one - pain, joy, and the entire range of needs experienced by an individual is felt by everyone. When unity (peace, harmony) is destroyed or damaged, relationships are guided by compassion, the attempt to empathize with others. When compassion no longer guides relationships, justice without feeling or emotion prevails; that is, a legalistic abstraction of fairness, wherein an individual's uniqueness is ignored. Finally, when even justice without feeling no longer guides relationships, they are reduced to a complete "loss of self." When greed and materialism determine the extent and nature of relationship, everyone and everything in the world are reduced to the status of lifeless objects.

SACRED FIREPLACE

Petega Yuha Mani praying during marriage ceremony

LIFE TEACHINGS & EXPERIENCES
One (*Wanji*)

LIFE TEACHINGS & EXPERIENCES

This is the winter of 1989, and I am seventy-seven years old. I am Pete Catches, Sr., known in the Indian world as *Petaga Yuha Mani* (He Walks with Hot Coals). I am an Oglala Lakota, born and raised on the Pine Ridge Reservation. I still live on the reservation, and hope to be here until the end of my life.

From these windows of seventy-seven years of life, I have watched the world pass before me. Many times, especially very early in the morning when I wake up, I lie awake and look back over the years to when I was a kid.

I was born to Paul and Anna Catches The Enemy at Manderson, South Dakota, which is located between Pine Ridge and Porcupine. My grandmother's name was Her Red Horses, and my grandfather's name was Big Ribs. At that time in the life of my grandfather and grandmother, most of the people did not have first names, but went by their childhood names instead. Many brothers and sisters had different surnames.

As a kid, I lived in Grass Creek, way back in the country between **Manderson** and *Oglala*. We had to go several miles to a spring that was cold in the summer. We would make a special trip to the spring on horseback to bring back cold water to enjoy in the heat. Nowadays, we don't have to travel so far for cold water. We have many things that make life easier for us that were absent from our early lives.

I lost both my father and mother when I was very young. I do not recall my *unci* (grandmother) or *kakala* (grandfather). But I did have an uncle who raised me, who advised me on how to live. When I was seven years old, he taught me when I got up in the morning to put on my clothing and then fix my bed - not to just get up, walk away, and let the blankets lie around. He taught me to take care of those things, because they kept me warm all night. That is showing respect and love for the things that you have, even a blanket. He told me that you take care of your cap, because you wear it through the day. He told me to show respect for my clothing by hanging it up, not to throw it here and there. Another thing he told me was that when I borrow something, I must show respect and be sure to return it.

My uncle taught me about pride in the Lakota people and about traditional ways. Long after the kerosene lamp was blown out at night, he would ask me, " *Tunska* (Nephew), are you awake?" And I would say, "Yes." Then he would begin talking about the things that came to mind, the things that were good for me to do. He said, "When you walk along to the neighbors on an errand, as you walk along the creek and there is a stick of wood, perhaps six or seven feet long you break off the other branches and carry that. When you come upon another one, you break off the branches and carry the length of it. You carry two or three, and when you arrive at the neighbor's on whatever errand you are on, take it to the woodpile. If you

LIFE TEACHINGS & EXPERIENCES

see an axe there. chop these branches to the length of a cooking stove. When you take a dipperfull of water to drink, if you see the water is getting low - usually there are two buckets there, maybe three - you take the one that has less water in it, pour it into another bucket, go outside to the barrel or the pump and bring in a bucketful for the household. In doing these small things, even though you are not told to do so, these people will be kind to you. They will see that you did not just go there to loaf or sit around."

My uncle said, "When I wake you in the morning, you get up. Do not have me holler at you a second time. When you hear my voice just get up. After you do that two or three times, it will become a habit. It will be easier for you to get up in the morning. But thinking that you will take another minute or so in sleep or lying down, taking it easy, and getting up slowly, indicates your laziness. So, when you hear my voice, just get up."

He taught me a lot of things. I went with him one morning to look for the horses. The lead horse - called the mother horse in our language, sometimes the oldest mare in a group of horses - has a bell around its neck, and they call them bell horses. He said, "This is what you do. That rope hanging by the side of the door, take that down and follow the trail to the hill. Just follow behind me."

As we walked along and came to the crest of the hill, he said, "What you do next is listen good for a time, a space of time, and wait until it is calm, and then holler out loud, as loud as you can. The bell horse, over there in the canyon or wherever, will hear you and move, and you can hear the bell. Follow that sound and you will find the horses. So, early in the morning when you get up on the hill, you stand there listening. You may barely hear that bell because in the morning, whether they are lying down or standing up, they are asleep. But if you can hear that bell, you can follow the sound and find where the horses are."

In that group of horses was one whose coat was an odd color. We called him by his nickname, *Sihanskala*, which means "long feet," because his back hooves were kind of slender. When he walked, you could see the tracks - it seemed as if somebody in moccasins went through there. I would go up to him, talking all the while, and he would just stand there. He loved to be talked to and petted. I would pet him all over, even down to his feet. He would look down to his ankle and he would be looking at me, his head over the other way, but still looking at me. I would also pull on his tail; he liked that too. He would turn his head one way or the other, showing his pleasure. Finally, I would put my rope around his neck, lead him to the side of a hill or to a little bank somewhere, find a place there, and jump on top of him. Then we would bring the other horses to the watering place in the canyon, water them, and take them to the corral. By that time, the sun would have risen.

All of this work would happen in the morning before sunrise, and I got used to that. I loved to be outside before sunup to inhale the freshness of the air, to be able to wake up the birds. Many times I was out there on the trail before they started singing.

My uncle taught me about paying attention. He said, "Be obedient. When you go someplace, to a neighbor's, see what the woman of the house is doing. If she is cooking, go to the woodpile, and if there is no cut wood, try to cut some. If you cannot

LIFE TEACHINGS & EXPERIENCES

cut wood, get some wood chips, a bucket of chips, and replenish her fire. See what else you can do." In this way, my uncle told me, "people will love you - they will know that you are eager to help."

So, that is how I started my life, Later, when I went out to work on a ranch or on a farm, I would ask to do more than what I was allotted. If I were driving a tractor, plowing a field, or feeding cattle in the wintertime, I would ask to milk the family cow or feed the chickens or the hogs. I spent long hours going out of my way to do the chores of the family farm or the ranch, besides the work I would normally do each day.

I worked seven days a week on some jobs. I worked on one particular ranch for several summers. I volunteered to make the rounds of the windmills on Sunday mornings, take salt out there in a pickup. If I remember right, there were seventeen windmills on that ranch. Even though some repairs were needed around the windmills, I could not get to all of them in one day. So I would continue my work the following Sunday. Some Sundays I would mount a horse and ride the outside fence, checking it. If I saw a break in the fence, when I returned the next week my first task would be to go and repair it.

My uncle also taught me to be honest and to be kind. He taught me how to be generous. He said, "Generosity is not just giving; generosity is sharing. Generosity to me is visiting the sick when you have other things to do, but you put that aside and go visit the sick. That to me is the greatest generosity, to put aside some thing you should do and go visit the sick." I have done this many times throughout my life.

SACRED FIREPLACE

Instead of having an *unci*, a grandmother, I had my uncle to teach me many good things in life. He told me, "Never try to imitate somebody; just try to be you. Live in this world the way *Wakan Tanka* (the Great Spirit), *Tunkasila* (Grandfather), fashioned for you to live, because you can never be what you are not. Even though you try hard to be what you are not, you will never be what you were not made for."

As I grew up, I began to understand these words. "Do not try to be what you are not." Those very small words are very strong. One of the things he taught me was that I would never be a white man, a *wasicu*, so I should not be imitating the white man's way. Even though I eat his food and use his way of clothing, forever and ever I will be a Lakota, because I talk Lakota, and I live the Lakota way. I am a medicine man, and the white man cannot ever be what I am. He may learn how to talk Lakota. He may try to imitate me by living the Lakota way, but never in this life, in this world, will he be a Lakota like I am.

These are the things my uncle taught me. I did not fully grasp the meaning, the full meaning, of what he taught me until later on in life. When I was a young man, during the time he was still teaching me, he too passed away. Looking back, I wish that I could have lived side by side with him for many years before his final end. His name was William Cedar Face. He was very well known. He was very expressive when he talked Lakota. So I had an Indian, a Lakota, training and teaching me, and I think I still keep parts of these things in my life today. My belief is like that.

LIFE TEACHINGS & EXPERIENCES

Traditionally, the family circle - what we know as *tiyospaye* (community) - provides security for people in Indian culture. In Indian families, children are naturally bashful. To other people who may come as visitors, it might seem as if the children were backward. But within the family circle, we understood what unity was. We loved one another, we would come to each other, we helped each other, and we shared everything that we had. I have known instances where a family member was not present at the time we were fortunate to receive a small bucket of plums or cherries. We would see to it that a portion of the fruit was saved for the absent member of the family. Being a family for us means that all partake of what there is to eat.

When I refer to tradition, I am speaking of the Red Road of Life, the language that we speak, and the belief of the *Sacred* Pipe. We use this belief system to guide our lives. In comparison, in today's lifestyle that we know under this dominant society, everything is turned way around. Children now might not share with each other. I realize that children are thoughtless. If a family member is not with them at the time that they have ice cream or pie, many do not save a portion for the absent member.

How the world has changed under this dominant society! The sense of value, honesty, and truthfulness is gone from our people. Others may say that it is still here, but no. I see these changes happening not only on the Pine Ridge Reservation but also wherever I go on other reservations.

So much of our way of life is being lost. Honor and respect are two of the things that we Lakota hold in high esteem. For example, when we go to a wake, it is to pay our last respects. When I was a boy, I did not know what death was. Children were forbidden to go to a wake, and especially to a funeral. The old ones wanted us to live a long time and, during childhood, they did not want us to see them crying at a funeral. This is one tradition that is absolutely gone from our people today. You go to pay your respects nowadays and all you see are children running around without supervision. Their mothers and dads are there not noticing. Children go out the door and the next minute they go back inside as though it was a recreation area; they are practically stepping on your toes. At the cemetery you will see children standing right there at the gravesite, looking down at the coffin being lowered into the hole.

    Why do we not show respect by keeping our children at home? People may see this in other, nontraditional ways. They might say, "We want them to get used to these things." But this I did not know when I was a child. This is not the Lakota way of showing respect for the old ones.

    I look back on the world that we had. All the streams that flowed through the country were clean and pure, there were virgin forests, and the snow-capped mountains were clean and pure. But after the cry of "westward ho," the white men took, and took, and took. Even now, they are after the Black

LIFE TEACHINGS & EXPERIENCES

Hills, the only remaining sacred Black Hills that we have, which are protected by the Treaty of 1868.[6]

It is very sad for me to contemplate the issue of the Black Hills. A treaty is supposed to be the highest law of the land. We have had many treaties with the United States government and the government broke every one of those treaties. If they break the Black Hills 1868 Treaty, I think the United States government has no face, no honor, no dignity. We are the aboriginal people of this vast Turtle Island. We are the original people, the landlords. The loss of our land undermines all that we hold dear. The sacred Black Hills are not for sale.

On Religion

I heard one old-timer say that we are gradually being divided through so-called Christianity and education. My early education was at Holy Rosary Mission, now known as Red Cloud Indian School. It was a Jesuit- and Franciscan-run boarding school located on the Pine Ridge Indian Reservation. I attended that school for a number of years. There were many misunderstandings and misconception when I was in school and there was a great culture

---

[6] The 1868 Treaty was broken by the discovery of gold in the Black Hills by an expedition led by General George A. Custer, after which the U S government annexed the land. Beginning in the 1920's, the Great Sioux Nation initiated litigation to have the government comply with the treaty. In 1980, the U S Supreme Court ruled that the broken treaty was "a rank case of justice," and awarded the Great Sioux Nation $119 million (described as market value of the land at that time of annexation, plus interest payments since that date). The money award was rejected by the Nation and at the time of this writing, the case was still in the courts.

clash. We came from Indian families, and when we went to school we did not know much about the English language. The only words we were familiar with were "yes" and "no." Sometimes we like to say "no" or we hollered out "yes" at the wrong time and in the wrong situations, and we would be punished.

The school teachers we had in early childhood were not kind. I would not say that they were racist, but rather that they were just plain mean to the Indian boys. I do not know about treatment of the girls because we were completely separated. The boys' section was on one side of the school, the girls' section on the other, and there was a high fence in between. We could not communicate with any of our female relations on the other side, and they, in turn, could not speak to us. There was no visiting of any sort. We were kept strictly apart. That is one of the reasons why I say they were mean.

The Indian boys who were sent to this boarding school were punished when they talked Lakota, our native language. We had long hair by the time school began in the fall, shoulder length or even longer. Many of us went back to school with long hair, uncut since spring, ever since school was out, and for that we got punished, too. As part of the punishment, we were cut bald-headed; it was very embarrassing for a boy to be bald-headed at that time.

I would say that religion, prayers, and the English language were forced upon me. They did not do these things in a kindly way. A young man taught us every day about a religion, about heaven, hell, and all that it pertains to, in order for us to become believers. Later on, I realized that I was brain-washed. As I grew older, I found that teaching religion forcibly is not a true Christian way of life. But in this Catholic institution, the beliefs about heaven and hell and purgatory and so on were forced into me, and I believed. Even today, I cannot get it out of my mind completely.

I do not understand the reason for the cruel things that they did. They supposedly lived by the Bible and the word of Jesus Christ, that Jesus Christ is the truth, the light of the world, and the way to live. A true Christian would be like Jesus Christ; he would be forgiving, and he would be understanding with sinners, so to speak. But these teachers were not that way. I think they were mean to us because we were Indians.

As a young boy in school, I saw pictures of the Pilgrims back in the 1600s. These Pilgrims were walking two by two, each man with his wife, going to church dressed in their best finery. The men had a Bible under one arm, and on the shoulder on the other side was a gun. That picture remains with me in my mind: this is America. They use that Bible sometimes to divide people.

When I came away from school, I tried to put the way they taught me in perspective in the world that I experienced in my adult life, working among white people in various states, including Colorado, Wyoming, and Nebraska. Another side of the picture in America is that we are human beings, that each person is an individual, that we can say the things that we want to say, that we can talk Indian if we want to. Why does this Christian institution try to curb all of that? They wanted to do away with our way of life, our culture, our traditions, our language. They wanted to stamp all of that out and make us into something that we know very little of.

One of the treaties signed by the Lakota Nation said that only three denominations were allowed in the Lakota Nation: Presbyterian, Episcopalian, and Roman Catholic. Today we have close to 100 churches in Indian country. I see religion as the system used by the United States government and the church, no matter what denomination, to divide the people. Brothers are divided with this church thing. There are so many churches that Indian people believe in many ways.

I see some people go to church every Sunday, and those same people hate other people. Some of those people who go to churches do not like me when they see me in the street, because I pray with the Pipe. They look at me as an enemy. This Lord Jesus Christ that they believe in, I believe in Him, too. But I believe in Him in a different way. I believe in Jesus Christ as the greatest of Medicine Men. He said in the Bible to love your neighbors and love your enemies.

I am not saying that these churches are no good. I like a person when he prays, no matter how he prays; and it is the same Creator that all the rest of us pray to. So in a sense, these people are all good, but only if they do what the Bible preaches, what the Bible says. I see the answers in the Bible. I have read the Bible. John the Baptist preached the coming of Christ in the desert wearing a camel's hide. In that desert heat, he lived on locusts and honey. How many of us could do that for our God? There are other great men of the Bible, like Moses on Sinai. He went up there to pray for forty days and forty nights. The Indian people look on Moses and they say openly that he went on a fast like we do with our Pipe. We go on a fast, but not as long as forty days. The longest we go is four days and four nights because, to us, the number four is sacred. The numbers seven, fourteen, and twenty-eight are sacred to us too.

It is very hard to live a traditional life. We eat the white man's food, wear his clothes, speak his language. When I talk English, I hate myself. I would rather talk Lakota because that is how *Wakan Tanka* made me. He made me for what I am. He gave me a language, a tongue to pray to Him, to talk to Him. He gave me ways to worship Him; that is love and I know He loves me.

How is it that ages and ages ago - and no one had to tell us this - the Indian people knew there is a *Wakan Tanka*, a Great Spirit, whom other people call God. Our *Wakan Tanka* is right here as I talk. He is right here listening to what I am saying, so He knows that what I am saying is the truth. In the message that is going out to the world from this moment, I ask *Wakan Tanka* to bless those people that receive it, and learn something from it, that maybe even one word from it will cure people of the problems they have.

The Great Spirit's Guiding Hand

Now I will turn to some happenings that occurred at various times in my life. Earlier in my life, I was sometimes active in local rodeos, like the ones at *Oglala* on the Fourth of July, Manderson on the

SACRED FIREPLACE

Fourth of July, the Kyle District Fair, the Custer Gold Discovery Days, and the Pine Ridge Oglala Sundance. They had races and rodeos, and I took part in bareback riding in most of the Pine Ridge rodeos. I could have continued in the rodeo circuit if I were not so poor. It takes money for entrance fees, travel, meals, expenses, and I did not have that.

At the time I am talking about, in the late 1930's through the early 1950's, money was hard to come by. You could not find a job during the Depression. A person who wanted to go to a rodeo had to sell his horse or some part of his property, like a saddle, in order to get there. I did not have that kind of stuff. So, I just participated to a small extent, but I loved it.

I got injured once at the Kyle District Fair. The horse I was riding seemed to understand when the whistle blew that the ride was over. When the whistle blew, he quit bucking and took off at a run. He was a fast runner. I started to get off; I slung my right leg over the side of the horse. At that moment I heard someone coming. There was a rider on a gray horse. He said, "Stay on and I will pick you up." I believed him. So, I remained sitting sideways on that fast-running horse. I was constantly sliding back towards the tail, towards the rump of that running horse. I realized the guy that was to pick me up was losing ground. When the chance was good, I braced myself and jumped off. I landed on my right leg, and I somersaulted several times. When I got up, there was a sprain to my knee, and the lower portion of my leg from the knee on down was in front of me, and it was going every which way. It would not stand still, so I grabbed hold of it.

LIFE TEACHINGS & EXPERIENCES

That injury lasted quite a while. The local doctor, a Dr. McNeil, who was living in Kyle at that time, doctored me. People knew and liked him. He was sort of an old man, but very successful in what he did. People liked him. He set my leg in place. Once you wrench the knee joint like that, only the person who experiences it knows the agony and pain that goes with it. The doctor gave me a handful of pills, but they did not help. I had to resort to cheap whiskey, called moonshine, to help me deaden that pain. I did not sleep that night, and I did not sleep the following night because of the pain. That is the only time I ever got hurt real bad in the rodeos.

Until a few years ago, I have broken horses or trained them, both in harness and saddle. In fact, we had a bunch of horses at the time I was riding rodeo. We had over thirty head that we took care of at the home place. I would bring two or three back for those people that wanted me to break their horses. I like to talk to them. I like to be kind to them, feeding them, petting them, and giving them sugar.

When I brought a wild horse back to the home place, people used to say that it would head back for home. But the horses did not return home when I turned them loose. I would tell them, "Stay around here. This is like your home." I would say this to the horse in Lakota, speaking my language. The horses got to know me pretty well, and they would stay.

I loved to work among horses. The last time one bucked with me on its back was when I was sixty years old. It is the custom in a family circle that one has to ride out to gather horses early each morning.

SACRED FIREPLACE

One Easter Sunday morning, during the time that I worked for the church, we had to go to church later because of what happened with this horse.

Early in the morning, I went to this ridge and I was riding a half-broke horse; his name was *Spaniciya* (Burnt Himself). I was loping along this ridge, looking this way and that way, searching for the horses. When I came to a point where I was to turn around I slowed down, and just about that time my stirrup broke. And of course, when this half-broke horse saw the whole stirrup flying out to one side, he started bucking in a circle, right on the tip of this ridge.

On each side was a sloping hill. When he went up, out, and cat-fished, I thought he was going to sail over the side, but he kept his footing. Sometimes the dirt on the bank would give way under the weight of his bucking. Then he would sit down, practically falling over. Then he would get to his feet and start bucking again.

I did not fall off, but that was some ride. When the horse quit bucking, I calmed him down and talked to him. I saw my stirrup quite a distance away. It was lying halfway down the hill. I had to lead my horse over to the broken stirrup. When I finished repairing the stirrup, I went down into the valley to continue searching for horses.

This is part of the way of life that most Indians lived in those days. We did not have to ride in a rodeo. We did not have to have a crowd cheering. That morning when this half-broke horse was jumping under me and turning this way and that way, bucking in a circle, nearly falling down, the only observers at the scene were birds. Maybe the

LIFE TEACHINGS & EXPERIENCES

Great Spirit reached out His protective hand. This incident was not the only one. I have experienced many more. I know the Great Spirit was there watching over me, even in my foolishness, to see that later on in my life I could be of some use to the people whom I live with in this world.

In many instances in my life, like the one I just related, we had to get to the church at a given time and time was running out. I had to get the horses, search for them, and run them back to the corral. We traveled by wagon and team in those days. But we got to church on time, no matter what, under any circumstances, rain or shine.

Sometimes you run for time, sometimes you get late, or you get bogged down because of something that broke. But all in all, it is the work that really counts, the efforts that you make. It is our belief that as a person you look at the future with faith in yourself. Knowing that you have set a goal to that point in your life, the road that you take, you realize is much harder than you thought, but having the will to continue is what counts.

Now I will talk about certain happenings in my life. I sometimes like to remember these episodes, because it was a time when people knew me for what I could do. I was never a bragger; I only talk the truth. These happenings were not sacred things, although you can look at them that way. I know the Great Spirit in His mysterious ways takes care of His people. And by that, I mean that He took care of me. He had a plan for me, a pattern of life. What I am doing is what He intended me to be in my life, a medicine man of the people, of the Oglala Lakota people.

SACRED FIREPLACE

When I was seventeen years old I was working on a farm picking corn. I was privileged to use a team of mules that belonged to this farmer. The whole outfit was the farmer's property: the wagon, the harness, and the team of mules. There were a couple of other Indian camps there, and they, too, were picking corn. One evening, I had chores to do at home at the camp. Because we lived in tents and this was in the month of January, it was cold. I had to chop wood for the evening, night, and early morning, and perhaps the next day. So, it was part of my work to come in from the fields early in the evening so that I could chop wood.

This one particular evening, I came in with the team of mules. I unloaded my load. I could not pick much corn since this was the first year that I did any kind of farm work. I had picked potatoes that fall, and then we started picking corn in December. "Shucking corn" is what they say. You take the outer covering of the corn and you break it off and throw the naked corn into the wagon box. Some people are good at it. They would get a load or nearly a load before noon, and by the evening they would get another. But, being my first year picking corn, I only picked about fourteen, fifteen, or sixteen bushels in half a day. The farmer was paying ten cents a bushel. It was a decent wage that accumulated in a week.

So, I came in early that one particular day. I unloaded my load of corn, took the team of mules to the water tank to drink, and then I took them to the barn. The first stall belonged to the team of mules. I put the mules in their stall, and I took the harnesses off and hung them on the wall. When I was through, I heard a wagon come in. I went outside and saw workers from one of the other Indian camps who had come in early because they had a load. I went to the driver and said, "You go ahead and unload your load and I will take care of your team." So he said, "All right," and he started unloading his corn. I unhitched his team and took them to the watering place.

After the team was finished drinking water, I led them into the doorway to the barn near the mules. I walked in, and the mules were feeding on the oats, I guess they did not want to be bothered. The mules heard horses coming in with harnesses jingling and making noise, and they knew it was horses. In their animal way, they did not want horses to come near them, maybe feed on what they were eating. So I heard something whistling like a strong wind, whoosh, just like that. I turned my head just in time to see one of the mules kicking with both hind hooves. They missed my face by maybe two or three inches beside me, one on each side of my face.

I could not sleep that night, thinking that if I was just a bit to one side, my head would have been smashed against the wall. The mule had backed up; it gave a forceful kick, raising his whole hind end, and kicked out with both legs. His hooves were in line with my face, and the hooves hit the wall. I did not want to go to bed. I even thought that if I went to sleep, I would die. Maybe it was what they refer to as shock.

SACRED FIREPLACE

Petaga Yuha Mani praying with his Pipe to the Great Mystery

Two (Nunpa)

ON BEING A MEDICINE MAN

BECOMING A MEDICINE MAN

Through the years, many people who are interested in what I do, and some who are skeptics for whatever reason, always ask me this one question: "What is it that makes you a medicine man? What is so special about it?" And sometimes they ask, "Is that the only thing you can do?" I always answer in the way that I am going to talk about now, about certain portions of my life as a medicine man.

I finally became a medicine man sixteen years after I was supposed to. I first had a sacred dream that I could not dispel. It was before me, it was in back of me, it was all around me. I could not sleep right; I could not eat right. It haunted me. I dreamed that I danced the Sundance. I was the lone dancer.

In the Lakota way, you are supposed to act out a sacred vision. But I did not want it. In fact, I tried hard to avoid it. Why I did not want it is very simple to understand. I hated it because I was brought up in my early school days by the Jesuit missionaries. The missionaries infused in our minds that Indian ways, especially the doctoring and the Pipe ceremonies, were heathen ways. They said, "It is pagan worship and devil worship." Being young minds, we believed it. I believed it. That is why I had a difficult time for sixteen years, why I struggled to get away from my dream, to forget it.

This call of the medicine way of life was strong. It was close to me. It was in the meals that I ate. It was in my dreams, a constant reminder that I had to go that way. I even worked for the church for five years. But still that lingering thought stayed, wherever I was, whatever I was doing. Only when I was dead tired could I have a good night's sleep. I would walk and walk up in the hills way late at night and come in at midnight or later dead tired. I would lay down on the bed, my shoes and everything on, and go to sleep. I spent months at a time, working on ranches and farms in Nebraska, Wyoming, and Colorado. Just to forget, I worked like everything to tire myself physically so I could sleep well at night. I would seek out rough country or rough weather to dispel this feeling that was always close at hand, always close to me, whether I was doing ranch work or farm work, picking potatoes, working in a blizzard, going out to work when others would not want to. When I did irrigation work, I would go nineteen, twenty, twenty-one hours at a stretch, just so that I would be dog-tired when I went home. Sometimes, without even eating anything, I would just flop on the bed and go to sleep.

In trying to avoid becoming a medicine man, I became part of the tribal council administration in the mid-1960s. I was a tribal cop on three occasions, to get away from this haunting thing that was always close at hand. I wanted to forget it all. Sometimes, I even drank alcohol and got drunk to

ON BEING A MEDICINE MAN

forget this sacred dream. But when I sobered up, it was still there, never to be blotted out.

Finally, I could not stand it anymore. So I thought to myself, "I will do this one thing that is part of the sacred dream, that I Sundance." In the Sundance dream, I was the lone dancer. That was the dream and it was a hard dream. Sometimes I hear people say they had a sacred dream. Then, after telling me their dream was dancing the Sundance, they would just go to a Sundance and dance it away. That tells me that their dream was not a sacred Sundance dream, because mine was so different from the way they dance nowadays. When I went to a Sundance, I would see six or seven dancers, and my dream did not fit that. I had to dance alone. Even this past year, in one Sundance there were, perhaps, a hundred dancers. But in the sacred dream I had, I was the lone dancer. Where could I do that?

So, the doing of it was a big problem. In my dream, only part of the Sundance arbor was whole and complete. The other part was just pine limbs stuck into the ground, and nowhere could I find a place like that. In the sacred dream, I danced only one day but I pierced in the morning, remained pierced all day and all the while I danced, I was crying. Because of this, it was doubly hard for me to fulfill this dream of mine. That is another reason why I kept postponing it for sixteen years.

Finally, on July 7, 1964, my family and a few other families got together and I fulfilled my sacred dream at a place known to us as *Pte Woku* (Feeding of the Buffalo). I thought I was going to dance and get it over with. We fixed that arbor just like in my dream. One thing that frightened me is

SACRED FIREPLACE

that all the time that I danced, I was crying. In the many years since then, even in Sundances that I directed, and I have directed eight consecutive Sun - dances at Little Eagle on the Standing Rock Reservation, I have never seen a dancer who danced and cried all the way through. I wondered why was I crying all day? I was at the height of my manhood; I was a strong man. But when we went to get that Sundance tree, it fell on my leg and busted it. I had to dance on that busted leg all day. That was why I was crying all that day in my sacred dream. As in the dream, I pierced in the morning. Nowadays, I go to Sundances and see people Sundancing. I do not see any of them crying. Mine was different. Mine was hard to do. There was no play-acting; it was the real McCoy.

On that day I stood pierced beneath the tree, and I was fighting, fighting to break free. There was a huge thunderstorm building in the west with very dark clouds, very close and low upon the horizon. Our people have a word for this kind of sky, *maka mani ukea* (close and on the ground it comes). There were some white clouds coming in between, some going up and some coming down. People were scared - they wanted to get away, since this was out in the rough country. The roads were hard to get through even when they were dry, and when it rained no car could come out of there. So, before it rained, they wanted to get back to the highway. Big drops of rain fell here and there, making a noise like hitting the ground. People were very anxious to leave. Some even got up and were walking toward their cars.

I called for my Pipe as in the dream, and when the Sundance helpers brought it to me I said the words that I dreamed to part that storm. I started praying. I pointed that Pipe to the advancing thunderstorm. You could hear the thunder, deep and heavy. It was close by, just about reaching us. I parted that thunderstorm in the center. Part of it went north, and part of it went south. The Sundance helpers watching the storm said that there were some eagles flying way up high, above the parted thunderhead. The part of the thunderhead that turned north went around by the White River country. It destroyed a lot of gardens and crops, and turned over a lot of outhouses, clear into the Kyle community area.

The thunderhead that turned south did the same damage in Pine Ridge and beyond. There was much hail and high winds. Our belief in our culture tells us that when the *Wakinyan* (Thunder Beings) come over the land, they bring water; they want to shake up the earth, bring it to life, and they bring water to give the thirsty earth. But when you direct them elsewhere they are *eyokipisni* (not happy), they say *chatkuta ukea* (from the back it comes), and they turn away and then reappear.

That is how it happened. In both directions, the thunderheads did a lot of damage, hailing out crops and tearing up trees. I continued my dancing. Only a few drops, heavy, big raindrops fell here and there on us, but that was all. We continued with the dancing until late afternoon when I broke free. When I broke free, my busted leg was healed and it seemed that peace had finally come to my spirit. My physical being was appeased with the thought that the Great Spirit heard my prayer. The sacred dream that had tormented me for sixteen years was finally over. It seemed that now I would live without torment, that I would live a good life knowing I had an obligation, and I had fulfilled that obligation.

But it was not to be. I went deeper into spirituality. By reenacting this sacred dream and doing the Sun-dance, I had accepted that I would live traditionally the rest of my life and become a medicine man. In four consecutive summers, I would give a thanksgiving Pipefast in fulfillment of this sacred dream.

You see what a sacred dream really entails - it is hard to do, and it frightens you. There is fear always, constantly with you and in you. It was there before me and every detail was in place. We fixed that arbor, just as in the way of my dream. The part of the dream that I thought would be very hard was for me to cry all the way during the Sundance. But when I did go through with it, that is exactly how it turned out to be. That dream and the reenacting of that sacred dream physically here on Mother Earth became one. That is how the power becomes real in a medicine man.

I recall now, after these many years, how tormented a period I came through, suffering physically. I should add spiritually, too, because in avoiding my dream, I did not even want to pray. It was so very real that even now, it makes me feel how small I am, how humble I am. In order to advance in the presence of the Great Spirit, one has to be humble.

Looking back over the years, I know what sacred means. It is something that we have to become worthy to approach, become worthy physically and spiritually, in order to fulfill some sacred thing. That Sundance dream was not the only sacred dream I

ON BEING A MEDICINE MAN

have had. I have had many sacred visions and my name is derived from one of these visions I had. It is *Petaga Yuha Mani* (Walks with Hot Coals).

The first summer, in 1958, that I went on a fast I had a vision. That vision was on the third day. I was standing in the heat of the summer day. Heat so strong and heavy, I did not know what the temperature was and I did not ask. I let it be how it was. So, standing there on the third day, weary, tired, thirsty, hungry, I held my Pipe up and it would gradually come down, and I tried hard to put it back up. And it would gradually come down, and I tried hard to put it back up.

You see, *Wakan Tanka* made me as I am and when I want to serve, I give it all that I have. So, I did not stand there with the Pipe resting on my stomach, or my elbows resting on my stomach. I held that Pipe up as high as I could and tried to hold it hours and hours at a time, because I wanted the Great Spirit to bless this Pipe. By blessing this Pipe, I wanted Him to bless me too, so that this Pipe and me would be like one, that whatever I did with this *Sacred* Pipe, the Great Spirit would listen. Many times throughout my life, I ask the Great Spirit to do something that is almost impossible, but being humble, being lowly, feeling unworthy, He grants me what I ask of Him. This is what makes me a medicine man.

So, I was standing there like that, raising the Pipe up there and singing a sacred song. When the Pipe was coming down, I noticed a man who was standing and facing the other way. In my vision, on the left side of the Pipe at a distance perhaps twenty, twenty-five yards out there, this man turned right and crossed over the Pipe. And when he did, there was a huge fire burning where he was going. He stopped short of the fire, knelt down, and took some sticks aside. He reached underneath and raked forth some hot coals. Then he cupped his hands, took a double heaping handful of hot coals, and he started to get up. He turned the other way, went very slowly around the fire and everything. The scene that I was seeing disappeared. This was the vision.

When I came back from the fast, I related what I had seen on that third day to the medicine man who was taking care of me. He did not know what to make of it and he said, "This is meant for you alone. It is not meant for me to tell you. This is meant for you alone and you will know yourself what it means."

About a year afterwards, a man came to our home. He said, "My father is very sick. I want you to come and doctor him. I was to bring you a Pipe but knew that if I brought that Pipe and you were not here, that will be a sure sign that my father is in a bad way. So, in order to be sure, I came alone. When you get there, I will offer you that Pipe."

When I came close to the dwelling, I could tell that they were smudging the inside of that house because I saw smoke coming out of the open doorway. I went in, and to my left was a cookstove with a burning fire. This was in the afternoon and there was a kettle of water that was steaming. When I went in, the man that came after me took a chair and placed it in front of his father's bed so I sat down facing the sick man.

ON BEING A MEDICINE MAN

The son came around in the back with the Pipe and offered me the Pipe. He lit the Pipe for me. I sat there, offering the Pipe to the Four Directions, and up above, and down to the earth. I sat there smoking, and I could feel the heavy gaze of someone looking at me. While I was smoking, I opened my eyes and looked at the old man. He was really staring at me and I could tell there was concern in his eyes. I could read his thoughts. He was thinking, "What is this son of a bitch trying to do? Does this son of a bitch think that he can cure me?" He had that on his mind. Because I had the *Sacred* Pipe in my hand, I was able to see his thoughts. I continued smoking until I was through.

In the group of people gathered there, there was one person, a close friend of mine who knows my altar, who knows the way I do things, the way I do doctoring. I called him over. "Get some cedar," I said, "and get a sweetgrass braid and crumble it together; mix it up. Hold it in your hand, and when I nod to you, come and help me." He went and got these things together. I got up and I walked as in the vision that I had seen. I walked slowly to that fire, to that stove. It was a wood kitchen stove with the fire box door in front. I opened it, and there was a large amount of hot coals there. I reached in there and raked forth hot coals like what I had seen in the vision, and took two heaping handfuls. Then I went slowly, turned around, and slowly went around and came back to where I was sitting. I nodded to my helper. He rushed forth and put the cedar and the crumpled sweetgrass on to the hot coals. This is how I smudged that sick old man, and how he was healed.

SACRED FIREPLACE

And by this I knew, thinking back on the incident years later, that this *Wakan Tanka*, the Great Mystery, fashions our lives for us. And whether we are being foolish or not, He saves us from leaving this world. He wants us to do something in life - something good, something pleasing, something that is very enriching to be in harmony with our fellow man.

Another occasion was the Saturday before Easter of that year. I had a friend, Silas Left Hand Bull, working at Holy Rosary Mission as a secretary and bookkeeper at the time. I went to the mission and while I was there, he said, "I'm glad you have come, because I want to hire you to go to Chadron (Nebraska). I phoned over there to the greenhouse and they are going to prepare two sets of lilies for the mass on Easter Sunday at the church."

I agreed to go. At that time, you could buy gas at the mission gas pump. He gave me money and they filled the tank for me. The attendant checked the oil and gave me extra oil. I told Silas, "I will go home and get prepared and I will come early. We will start as soon as you are finished with your office work."

I went home and told my wife that we had to go to Chadron, that Silas bought some lilies for the altar for Easter Sunday Mass. My wife said, "Can I go along? I want to buy some things at the store." I said, "All right. That will be good. We will make it one trip." So, we came early to the mission. When Silas got off work, we went to White Clay, and took a cut-across through Beaver Creek. At the side of Beaver Wall, there is a road that cuts through to

ON BEING A MEDICINE MAN

Hay Springs, and one that branches to Chadron. We went through there.

It was late when we got to Chadron. We drove directly to the greenhouse. The light was on and we went in. Someone had the order all prepared, a whole bunch of lilies, two sets, for Easter Sunday Mass. The lilies were put in a pasteboard box so they would not get crushed and we put them in the back trunk. We went to a restaurant on the Main Street of Chadron for supper, and then my wife did some shopping.

We started out late and we did not want to have trouble on the road. The cut-across was a gravel road, but most of it was muddy. So, we took the paved route going through Hay Springs, Rushville, and then north to White Clay, Pine Ridge, and Holy Rosary Mission. There are lots of trees there and the road kind of winds around but it is a good highway.

On the way back, right at Border Creek, up ahead was a loaded semi. It was traveling slow. When I came to it, there was another car following me. I wanted to pass the semi, and it looked like a clear passage. Just when my front wheels were even with the semi's cab, my instinct made me step on the brake and slow down. And when the semi left my front end, the right front wheel blew. I swerved to the right and I stopped on the shoulder right away. The car that was following me saw all that happened. It was a state patrolman. He came up to me and asked, "What happened?"

"I had a blowout!" I said. "Just when you saw me slow down and the semi left me, I had that blowout." If I had continued on and passed, I would have been in front of that semi, a heavy, loaded semi, when I had the blowout. The patrolman asked me, "What made you do that?" "I do not know," I said. "Some instinct made me slow down, really put on the brake and slow down. Just as the semi passed my front wheel, had that blowout and turned my car to the right." Luckily, I had a spare tire. The patrolman in his goodness, took out his jack and turned his lights on. He waited while we jacked up the car and took off the wheel. Of course I did all the work because the patrolman was in his uniform and I did not want him to get muddy. But he was there all the time. He was eager to help. When we finished replacing the tire, he asked how far we were going. We said we were going close to thirty miles north of Rushville.

The patrolman then asked if we thought our other tires were good. "If not, I will follow you all the way." He was that good, he was trying to help us. So, after we were through, he followed us to Hay Springs before he went on, making sure that we were okay.

I will tell you of another instance of this sort. One time in Colorado, the family went to a Fourth of July rodeo. I forget the town, but we were working near Fort Lupton at the time. I had bought a car in Denver, and we were going to this rodeo. We took in the activities, let the kids have fun, and bought candy and ice cream for them.

Highways, in those times, were narrow. On the way back, there was heavy traffic. I saw this heavy truck approaching, and I did not know what made me do it, but just as we came face to face with this truck, I turned the steering wheel halfway around to

ON BEING A MEDICINE MAN

the right. We went off the side of the road. Just then, the left front tire blew out. If I had not done that, if I did not have the instinct to do that, we would have hit the side of the semi truck.

Occasions like this make me wonder, "Why? What made me do that?" As human beings, we do not see the future, what is going to happen in the next hour or on the road. Those times I did the right thing at the right time to avoid accidents. And in all of these instances, the following night I could not sleep. That time I had my whole family with me—my wife, myself, and my small kids. We all could have perished there. But, I wonder, and I know that the Great Spirit protects us in times like this. I wonder, and I know that the Great Spirit in His mysterious ways, protects us for a reason. That reason could be for us to seek out our lives, where we fit into this life, what we can do to help others, and help ourselves, to make this life worth living, to make it easier for ourselves and for others.

May the Great Spirit's love, and in His goodness, bless you. Those people who may read this book will be blessed by the Great Spirit. I pray He will implant in their hearts a love and compassion for the sick. If we can, each in our own way, and in according to our own means, be able to lend a hand to others, then we know that we live in the light of the Great Spirit.

Petaga Yuha Mani with his Pipe & eagle feathers at Sundance in 1968

Constitution of a Medicine Man

I will try to explain what a medicine man is, what makes him a medicine man. In my wanderings here and there as a medicine man, I have talked of it, but never what really constitutes a full account of what really constitutes a medicine man.

ON BEING A MEDICINE MAN

A medicine man first has to be honest with himself. He has to be truthful, and he has to be humble. *Wakan Tanka* (Great Mystery) works in many strange and mysterious ways. He calls upon the weakest to do a great thing. He calls upon the lowly, the poor man to do His handiwork, that of curing human beings who are sick.

Humility is such a great thing, one of the essential things. We medicine men do not jump to the center. We do not raise our hands and say, "Here! Here! Here I am!" We stay in the background. A true medicine man does not walk the streets showing himself. He stays out where he lives. Somebody who needs a medicine man will go search for him and find him there. This is the true way of a medicine man.

These medicine men that go from state to state in search of the things that they want to do are not medicine men at all. It makes me think back over the years. I saw an old movie one time. Somewhere in the West, there was this so-called medicine man in sort of a sheep wagon, drawn by a team of horses, with his medicine advertisement written on the side. One of the things I remember well was, "A sure cure for all ills and pains." He had medicine comprised of snake oil, crushed grasshoppers, and all of that. Everywhere we still have these kinds of medicine men. They go from state to state proclaiming their power, that they are able to do this and that. I often wonder: do these same medicine men that have traces of Indian in them, do they have in their hip pocket a bottle of snake oil or crushed grasshoppers, ants, or whatever?

SACRED FIREPLACE

So, a true medicine man has to be humble. He has to stay where he lives. He has to be known where he lives. He has to practice whatever he does in his own community. Those that live around him go to him and seek his help. This is the kind of medicine man I am talking about, not the moving kind, the fly-by-night sort of medicine man.

A true medicine man lives a simple life. He lives without a lot of fancy pleasures, and this makes him stronger. When I was younger, I made myself suffer. I brought suffering upon myself. Now, I look at other people in different areas, like the church people, ministers, and priests. I have watched and worked with many. You see, for five years, I worked for the church when I was trying to get away from becoming a medicine man. I saw some who did likewise. They omit pleasures like smoking cigarettes and eating candy. These are some of the common, easy things to avoid, but in a sense it adds up to a great deal.

I have been called to Hawaii on two occasions. The first time I went to Maui, the second time I went to Oahu. The second time I went there, a person called and invited me to his home. He was sitting there on a rug. He was barefooted and shaggy. He had a full, long beard. He said he was a holy man. There was a girl sitting on his left, there was a girl sitting on his right, and he was very talkative. He said, "I am a holy man. I had a vision, a great vision. I saw God, and He spoke to me." As he was saying this, he was smoking weed, smoking marijuana. He took a couple of puffs and gave it to the girl on his left. She took two puffs and gave it to the other girl. That made me mad.

ON BEING A MEDICINE MAN

I told him, "Listen you, if you spoke to God, you would leave the pleasures of this world alone. You would not even notice them. You would get away from them. You would, perhaps, go live up in the mountains, go without food all day long, fast from drinking water, instead of sitting there smoking pot with girls on each side of you... You make me sick. You and your kind make me sick. It is the thing that you are smoking that makes you hallucinate. You are make-believe."

I got up and walked away. He called me back and I said, "No! You live in another world, in a dopey world. I will have nothing to do with you!"

So, too, in the medicine man world, the real one, the real medicine man is not fat. He might be a sorry-looking guy. He is thin, he might be weak physically, but his spirit is very strong. This constitutes a medicine man. Those that go from state to state, carrying their snake oil and crushed grasshoppers, these kind of medicine men go after money. They live good but their work is not always beneficial; it does not help the people. Why they do this is hard to understand. What they do reflects on everyone. It reflects on me and I hate for people to think that I might be that way too.

A medicine man does not fight. He does not raise his voice in anger. He does not raise his fist in anger. He does not even own a rifle. But the *Tunkasilas* (the spirits, or grandfathers) that watch over him really do take care of him. I never experienced anybody coming up to me and slapping me or hitting me. If that ever happened, the Tunkasilas will do the revenge for me, even though I do not want them to. Even though I do not,

SACRED FIREPLACE

here is the thing that happens. Anybody having bad feelings towards me gets his payback in terms of bad luck or misfortune, so to speak. This happens over and over again. My wife understands this very well; she sees it. I do not like it. I do not foster this. I do not care for it. I would let things ride as they are, but it happens that I am not saying everybody has to be good to me. No, that is not the way. We are human and we have our bad feelings. I, too, have bad feelings. Sometimes my mind is so warped, you know, with watching the alcohol-related suffering that goes on. Things that happen from alcohol. Especially when I see a baby pass from this life through alcohol-related things. Some hurt, some anger comes into my being. Sometimes that bad feeling cannot be controlled.

I say to people in order to satisfy them that being a medicine man is the hardest thing a person can do because we did not go to medical school. Myself, I am very ignorant. I am lowly, I am humble. But still, I can doctor people and doctor them for mental problems, heart conditions, stomach conditions, ulcers, diabetes, and arthritis. I have doctored people with phobias and they got well. I have doctored people with eye problems and they got well. So, a medicine man is ignorant, because he has not gone through books and books of teachings and instructions and medical classes. Yet, with the power of the Great Spirit and with the dreams that he has, the supernatural things and the physical world, these two unite as one to give him a power.

A medicine man can pass his power on to his sons. I had four grandfathers in this world that we are in. One grandfather married into the Arapahoe

ON BEING A MEDICINE MAN

tribe, one grandfather married into the Cheyenne tribe, and one grandfather married into the *Oglalas*. We are formerly from the Standing Rock Reservation. *Hunkpapa* (one of the seven bands of the Tetons) is where we come from, Sitting Bull's band. But one of my grandfathers married into the *Oglalas*, and that is how we are here. One grandfather left and never came back. No one knows where he went. Maybe he was killed somewhere. No one knows. There is no history of it.

So, being a medicine man is hereditary. All of these four grandfathers of mine were medicine men. My father was a medicine man and he quit being a medicine man and joined the church. That is how he left this world; he died that way. I worked for the church at one time for five years, and I left the church and became a medicine man. Generation after generation, we pass on the heredity of medicine men. Of my two sons who are following me, one of them will become a medicine man when I leave this world.

On the other hand, being a Lakota chief is not hereditary. A chief must earn his status. The Oglalas nowadays, especially under this new setup, this tribal council way, we take so many cut-a-crosses. In one family, I will not mention the name, where there was a chief, the first chief could not pass it on through the clan, which is happening today. They call themselves chiefs but they have no status. So, out on the traditional reservation, here in the backwoods so to speak, we do not look to that family as being chiefs.

SACRED FIREPLACE

Becoming a chief has to be earned from childhood. There are many, many virtues that have to be shown and learned, such as generosity, kindness, having courage, having respect for oneself and for others, being wise, and being a leader. A leader must be a role model. A leader must have the trust of the people that he is leading. How can they follow him if they do not trust him?

I would say that most of the tribe here does not feel that we have a chief because that world is gone. We have young men that went to war but that too is not of the same status as compared with warriors of long ago. A warrior of that age and a soldier of today, they are both courageous, they have both done brave deeds. They have both won honors. But, being a soldier today means they have to pledge allegiance to the United States flag. There you have it. They are not working for the tribe; they are working for another nation. So, in that sense, they are warriors under another flag. They are not warriors under a tribal flag. We have to understand these things.

Becoming a chief is not hereditary but a medicine man can give his powers to the next generation. This is tradition. It has to be in the DNA, so to speak. This is the heritage that we have and nothing can change it. We can fool around like many do in many things, like the Sundance and the sweat lodges, but what we do the Great Spirit will bless or will not bless what we do - that is the main thing to think about.

In my work, the first thing I think about when people want my help is: do they really believe in this? In the years that I have worked as a medicine

ON BEING A MEDICINE MAN

man, I have seen people come to a medicine man only when they need one, and in between, they do not care for him. Only when he is needed, he is taken off that shelf, and they use him and then put him away. But there are also people that keep you in mind. They know what you are, they respect you and that makes you feel good. They know that you are a person, too. They know that you are hungry, that you are tired, just like any human being.

A medicine man will go all out like I do and do all he can to provide the services asked of him by the people, such as funerals, marriages, blessings, namings, even prayers. My wife knows. Many times on these marches that we have been doing, I would get home, and she knows how tired I am, not from the walking but from the great impact of the meaning of the marches, such as DADD (Dads Against Drunk Driving). There are just a handful of us marching the roads against drunk driving. How many dads are there on the reservation? Are all the rest of them alcohol users? Maybe some of them are drunk drivers themselves. Do they not love their children in the way they should love their children, to go out there on the road and walk for the sake of their children?

These things go through my mind. Are our children going to grow up to be young men and women and have this problem that we have in front of us, still here with us, or maybe much worse? So, during a march, when I pray on the road and when I sing sacred songs on the road, it drains a lot of energy from me. It drains a heck of a lot of energy from me. When I get home I am so tired - spiritually, not physically. I am not tired because of the

SACRED FIREPLACE

walking, but from the prayers that I say imploring the Great Spirit to help us.

If I could choose to live like an ordinary person, most certainly I would grab that chance, because a medicine man is not a happy man. The only time that he is happy is when he knows he has cured a patient, when he knows that he has cured a sickness. That in itself is reward enough. A true medicine man never asks for any fees. But that doesn't mean that you don't give him something for what you are asking. It has to come from your heart. If you don't, it falls back on the medicine man and he gets sick. There always has to be balance.

A medicine man lives as lowly as possible. When you see one, you will know he is a true medicine man because he is not of this world. He does not go to pow-wows, he does not take pleasure in life, he does not go to circuses, rodeos or anything. He stays at home. It is a lonely life. That is one of the great sacrifices he has to make. I wonder how many young bucks of today qualify to become medicine men. They think of it in terms of glory. It is not. That is not how I see it - it requires many sacrifices, such as fasting.

Through my years of being a medicine man, I have been called to work in many states, including Hawaii, Nebraska, Wyoming, Colorado, Montana, Idaho, North Dakota, South Dakota, in Rosebud country, Lower Brule and many other reservations. Above all, I work in my own community. A medicine man is not choosy; he goes where he is wanted. He is not a member of any organization. He is a spiritual worker. He can go anywhere where he is wanted and work with people that want to use him or need him. So, it is not a glory thing and it is nothing to brag about. The more years that you tie yourself to it, the more that you want to get away from it. It is a lifelong thing - you are a medicine man until your dying breath.

A Doctoring Trip to Hawaii

The first time I went to Hawaii, I went to Maui. When I was ready to go home, people just did not want me to leave. They even suggested I stay and make my home there. I told them that South Dakota is my home and where I was born, and that I would like to return to the people I know, to the people who are part of me.

As I said before, a medicine man cannot be choosy. He goes where he is called. And the second trip that I went to Hawaii was in March of 1974 was one such instance. I did not want to go back because of the difficult time coming away from there the first time. I got a phone call telling me that I had a ticket to Hawaii waiting for me in Rapid City, but I did not want to go. I was just about to forget it when I received a letter from the people who had sent the ticket, explaining why they wanted me there. The mother of the family that sent for me is my niece. She is married to a person who was in the Air Force and he was stationed in Oahu. They have two daughters and one son. The son is the youngest. He was six years old at the time. In the letter, they explained that their son was very listless, very sick, that he acted like an old man. He had lost interest in everything, including his friends,

SACRED FIREPLACE

and even playing. In a word, they wanted me to doctor him. One part of his father's family history is unusual. Little John, the sick boy, was the only son. Little John's father was the only son in his family, and in the grandfather's family the grandfather was an only son. This was also probably going through the minds of the family, that John was an only son of an only son of an only son.

When I read that letter, I packed up my suitcase and I started walking towards the highway from where I was living at Mission Flat. There was a fresh snowfall and the day was warm. Everywhere the snow was melting, creating a runoff. You could not walk anywhere without splashing, so I did not go by the road; I took a cut-across through the fields to reach Highway 18. In the Calico Community they call this place Mission Flat. I reached the highway and I started walking.

There I was, hitchhiking to Rapid City, carrying my suitcase. I was walking on this flat, and just about the time I was going to go down a hill, I heard a car slow down, right where our land touches the highway. I did not even look back. The car slowed down and stopped, and then it came on beside me. Someone held the door open. "Get in, Uncle Pete," he said, so I got in. It was a pickup so I threw the suitcase in the back and I got in the front. It was my nephew, Eddie White Wolf and one of his friends.

Eddie asked me, "Where are you going?" This is a very common question around our area. People always see me walking the highway. I am usually going to Oglala, Pine Ridge, or somewhere near for a ceremony or whatever. Since I was carrying my

ON BEING A MEDICINE MAN

suitcase, he knew I was going to a ceremony. So I told him I was going to Hawaii.

He thought I was joking, and said, "and walking too," and the two looked at each other. They did not believe me. "Really," he said, "where are you going?" "Hawaii," I said. "My gosh, let us turn around and go back," said Eddie. They lived just off the highway. "Let us turn around and go back and have some coffee; we are hungry," he said, "and then we will take you to Hawaii." They still were thinking I was joking.

We turned around and we went back to my nephew's house. They fried some hamburger and eggs and made some coffee. They invited me to eat and I did. I had my mind on Hawaii and the sick young boy. While we were eating, my nephew asked me, "Uncle, where are you really going?" "I told you, I am going to Hawaii. I have a ticket waiting in Rapid City," I said.

"Oh! Now we believe you," he said. "We will take you to Rapid City. We will take you to the airport and see when you can take off." I was glad of that. I got a ride all the way into Rapid City, which is about 160 miles away.

We drove to Rapid City that afternoon and went straight to the airport. Eddie inquired for me if I had a ticket there. The agent looked through the computer and sure enough, I had a ticket with an open date. I could go any day.

They said the next flight was not until the next day, so we drove back to town and got a motel room. We had supper and went to bed. The next morning, we got ready and by noon we reached the

SACRED FIREPLACE

airport. They did see me off. I guess when they did see me off, then they really firmly believed that I was telling the truth. Believe it or not, this is what actually happened. This is the way the *Sacred* Pipe works. All you need to do is have faith in it so strong and deep enough that you can take off on foot, depending on nothing else, asking for no favors from no one, but just take off and the *Sacred* Pipe will take care of you.

Hawaii is a paradise on earth sort of thing. Rich people go there to pass away the time of day, to enjoy the weather, the fruits, whatever Hawaii has to offer. "Aloha" is the going word. When visitors from the mainland arrive there, they are given a lei, a string of beautiful flowers placed over your neck. I arrived in Hawaii after 11 p.m. their time. As is always my custom, whenever I am deplaning or debusing or whatever, I keep my seat until everybody has stood in line and left. I am always the last one to get in line and follow the crowd. The other travelers on my plane all got one lei. When it came my turn, I had one upon another. I had seven leis around my neck. Oh, these people I was flying with, they really looked at me. They thought I was a freak or something. But anyway, that is what happened.

The family met me at the airport and took me home. They knew I was tired. We had a quick meal and went to bed. The next morning, we visited and they told me about the problem. Little John was in the army hospital for observation. From the x-rays, the doctors thought he was suffering from leakage of the heart. Surgery would be required to see if that was the problem. On the twenty-fourth of the month, Little John was to go to the army hospital for heart surgery.

ON BEING A MEDICINE MAN

So, they gave me a day of rest and I explained to them what I was going to do. We were going to go into a ceremony. I asked if they could bring Little John home for a ceremony and they said they could. I explained the essential things, that when they pray they should really mean every word that they used in their prayer and it should be a positive prayer. I also told them how to prepare for a ceremony. They needed to get colored flags, tobacco pouches, and food, because no ceremony is complete without a feast. Whether that feast entails just Kool-Aid and sandwiches, it is still called a feast. Every ceremony has to be followed by a feast. All of this is inclusive in the ceremony; **what you put out is perhaps what you get.**

That night we went into a ceremony. Friends of the family gathered there with them to help out. They brought food, fruit, or whatever they wished to the feast. And they came to help pray. In the ceremony I told the parents that there was leakage of the heart, that there was a hole in Little John's heart. I told them I would fix this up and it would not trouble him anymore. The way I explained it was that I am only an instrument of *Wakan Tanka*, the Great Spirit. I am only a part of the doctoring, and the Great Spirit and the spirits that are with me as helpers, they will do the doctoring. In that way, the x-rays will not show what previously showed, that the little boy had leakage of the heart.

I took a small drum with me that I carried in a suitcase to use in the ceremony. After the ceremony, we visited with the other people. They were glad to see me and were enthused about the ceremony and the singing. That was the first time a lot of them ever smoked from the Pipe. I told them,

SACRED FIREPLACE

"When you smoke the Pipe, the smoke represents the breath of the Great Spirit. So what you pray for, either to help somebody else or to help yourself, your prayer should be on your mind while you are smoking the *Sacred Pipe*."

Cansasa, Indian tobacco, is a very different sort of a tobacco. They work together, the *cansasa* and the Peace Pipe. I have seen people that use Bull Durham in their Peace Pipe, but I do not go for that. That was not the way when the Peace Pipe was brought to the Lakota people. The original way was the *cansasa* (the inner bark of the red willow), and that is how it should be. It is traditional when you use *cansasa* in a Pipe. Well, the first time they smoked it after the ceremony was completed, they all liked the flavor of the *cansasa* in the Pipe, and they were really enthused by all of this.

The following morning was the time the family was to take the young boy to the army hospital. I used to remember the name of that hospital and the important places on Oahu, Maui, the extinct volcano, and all the popular places, but it has been years since. I should have written those names down but I did not. I lived each day as it presented itself. I had never intended that someday I would try to recall the names of places that I went to. So, I lost recollection of those names.

I do remember that the army hospital was situated on a hillside and all the buildings were pink. It was very beautiful. We took Little John there, the whole family and me, to the army hospital. That day, the boy was to be given another examination, pre-surgery, I think it is called. When they did examine

ON BEING A MEDICINE MAN

him, the x-ray films came out negative and the doctors could not believe it. They took the old film and compared the two. Looking at them, the two were completely different. The old one showed leakage of the heart and the new one showed nothing. Nothing was wrong. Little John went through a physical again, the x-ray part. But still it came out as before. There was nothing wrong with the boy.

They kept him overnight, and the following morning they x-rayed him again, for the third time. He was free from leakage of the heart. So, he was released. We went after him and took him home.

From the time of the ceremony up to the time that we brought him back from the hospital, there was a great deal of difference in Little John's attitude. His listlessness was gone. He had acted like an old man when I first saw him. He was sitting there with a bowed head, like he had given up all hope. That was gone. He was lively, he was smiling. He was like his old self.

At the supper table, when we were through eating, I talked to the father and the mother. The kids had finished eating and were in another room, so they did not hear. I had the father and mother remain there and I talked to them. I said, "This does not mean that Little John is completely well. No, what the spirit helpers did was cover up that leakage. They covered it up so the x-ray could not show how it was before. But when I get back to South Dakota, and when the snow falls on the country where I come from, then Little John will be completely well. But from now until the first snow in South Dakota you must never punish this boy, no

SACRED FIREPLACE

matter what he does. Never spank him, never scold him. He is going to be a rascal. He is going to make you feel that anger come to you. But remember, this is the consequence you must face. If you do not scold him, if you do not whip him, he will become completely well by the first snowfall in South Dakota."

The next morning, Little John was up on the roof. Oh, heck, it could get any mother frustrated. It could get any father red in the face. But they coaxed him down. Before the day was over, he broke the back windshield of their station wagon. By gosh, he was a rascal, climbing trees like a monkey. This was in March, so all through that spring and summer, they had a mischievous little son who was everywhere, like Dennis the Menace in the cartoon. It was that way for the length of time just as the spirits said it would be. But that was the consequence of this healing.

This little boy, six years old, was into everything. He would break dishes and everything else. I guess he was worse than Dennis the Menace. It seems like he was wise talking too and he had things to say that taunted his parents. When I left, he was still roughing it up, making misery for everybody. But he was healthy. He was putting food away, he was sleeping good, and he was doing somersaults and all of that you would think a person with leakage of the heart would not go through. He was going to show his parents that Indian religion, Indian healing, works.

I got letters from Little John's mother after the following winter, saying that he was periodically examined at the army hospital, but never a trace of this leakage of the heart ever appeared again. He is a young man now, and he is married. With the last word I received from the mother was that he is married and he has a family and a job.

When I hear of things like this, the result of something I did, that I was a part of the instrument of the working of the Great Spirit and the *Sacred* Pipe, it makes me all that much more humble. And I wonder sometimes, how does it work? I do not know myself. But it does work, and Indian people live in it and by it. Oh, we have hard knocks too; we have problems too. But I am sure that the problems we have are very trivial compared to our everyday problems if we were not in this so-called Indian religion.

Everything has a balance in this world - everything! There is a balance in this healing. It is not always the sort that I mentioned here. There are other consequences that could follow in the wake of a healing. So, here again I will say Indian religion is unique. It is a religion all by itself, very different from all other religions. We must, in this religion, have faith. That is the going word.

I have heard people say they go to this and that doctor and they cannot be cured, and that they will try this and that. There is no faith in such thinking, such as "I will try this Indian medicine way." More often as not, this "trying thing" does not work. You have to believe in it. It does not mean you have to believe to be a member of something. No. Heck no! Do you believe in a pill, in an aspirin to cure your headache? You know it is going to cure your headache. There you have it, there is that belief, a faith about something that will make you whole, that will cure you.

This is how Indian religion works. It is unique, it is something that *Wakan Tanka* gave to us. We do not need x-rays, modern techniques, the latest in modern powerful drugs to cure our ills. No, we ask the Great Spirit, the Creator of all things, to make us whole, to cure us. His Word is medicine. His Word is healing. Sometimes I wonder. We are truly the children of the Great Spirit because He watches over us, He takes care of us, and I know He loves us.

PRAYING AT DIFFICULT TIMES

In every person's life, there comes a time when they reach their prime. It may happen at any age, when they get to be the strongest, or when they get to be the heaviest. This sort of thing happened to me.

In the summer of 1969, I conducted two Sundances, one at Spring Creek on the Rosebud Reservation, and one right here on the Pine Ridge Indian Reservation. My weight was 206 pounds and I was healthy. I was strong. In the early winter of that year, in January, we were living in a cabin below a hill. The main hill runs sort of southwest to northeast. There is a branch in the ridge that reaches out to the right, or towards the east. It was below this point that my wife and I had a little cabin. There was deep snow on the ground and prior to this time I was talking to my oldest brother, Joe.

ON BEING A MEDICINE MAN

He was telling me about prayer. He said, "The Great Spirit is everywhere. He is in the room with you. He sees and knows what you are doing. Because He is always near, He knows your every action, your every deed. We should always be aware that the Great Spirit is always nearby, sometimes to help us, sometimes to just watch over us, sometimes to see what goes on in our minds."

My brother told me, "When the Great Spirit is nearest to you, that is the time to talk to Him. When the going is rough and tough, when trials of life are hardest to meet, that is the time to talk to the Great Spirit. I do not care where it is because that is the time He is closest to you."

I always remember what else my brother said: "No matter where you are...when you are lying underneath a car, lot of times your wrench slips, you hit your hand on the frame or some part of the car, you go to cussing around...or riding along on horseback, something spooks the horse and you go to bucking, and when something does not go the way it should. I do not care where you are, whatever you are doing; He is there beside you. When misery or problems assail you and the going is tough, that is the time to pray to Him. That is the time to talk to Him, because that is the time He is closest to you." So I feel this way.

One day I was thinking of what my brother told me. That night we were without food. We had very little. We were out of coffee, sugar, and some essential things, and we practically went to bed hungry. I was thinking about what my brother was saying, "When the going is tough, that is the time

SACRED FIREPLACE

you should talk to Him." I intended to go up on a hill to pray. So, I waited.

Later that night, my wife went to sleep. Way past midnight, I got up. I started putting on my shoes and my overshoes because there was a strong wind blowing outside and the snow was ten or eleven inches deep and drifts were even deeper. When I was putting on my jacket, my wife got up and asked me what I was doing. I told her, "You know what my brother was telling us one time, that when the going was tough that we should talk to the Great Spirit. Because when it is the toughest, that is the time He is closest to you." She said she remembered. "So, I am going up the hill, up to the very top, against the wind, and pray." She said, "All right, don't be gone long. Do not stay up there too long."

I opened the firebox to the heating stove, put a few more logs in it, and then I went outside. I took the outhouse path which was cleared and from there on, was deep snow. It was in high drifts in some places. I was headed for the point of the branch that fingers out towards the east. I had a difficult time climbing up to that point. I was among pine trees, so the going was all right. There were only gusts of wind and the swirling of snow. I slowly followed the ridge way. As I have said, in every person's life there comes a time when he is in his prime of life. I was at that point, 206 pounds. I was strong and heavy. I followed that ridge way slowly, going around boulders. Sometimes, I had to turn around and face downwind because the wind was getting stronger as I ascended to the top. I would catch my breath and then turn and go again. Finally, I came to the top.

ON BEING A MEDICINE MAN

After I reached the top, I knew what my brother Joe was talking about, "when the going is toughest." There I was, at a point when the going was toughest. I came from a home that was close to minus in food. I was all alone up there on the hill; it was way past midnight and the rest of the world was asleep. Strong gusts of wind staggered me. But I braced myself, and took out my Pipe, facing the wind. I remember what I said. "I want many more like this, *lena ota makuye*." I never thought what those two or three words meant. The meanings are so numerous. It means suffering, it means problems, problems that come in many forms, in many ways, sometimes every day, and far into the night. So, I prayed up there, and I remember those words, "*Lena ota makuye*."

I finished my prayer. I sat down and tried to light that Pipe, but I could not. There was no lighter or no match that could hold the flame long enough to puff on that Pipe, no matter what effort I put into it. So, I retreated downhill. I came around a boulder; I stopped there and wondered if I should try there. All along that finger of ridge pointing towards the east, I tried several places to light that Pipe, but I could not light it. In my mind, I wanted to be alone because I was talking to the Great Spirit. Any effort that I put into lighting that Pipe would not work. When I tried to light that Pipe, the flame would just flicker and go out. So, I went directly home, opened the firebox, got a coal and placed it on the bowl, and I went back up to that point on the ridge where I had come down.

I went back up there, sat in the snow and smoked my Pipe. I felt at peace. It is hard to explain. I finished smoking that Pipe and I started downhill again. It must have been easily two o'clock. By that time, my going back and forth made a trail, so going back down the last time was easier.

I got back inside the cabin, which was warm and good, and cleaned my pipe and put it away. I sat in a chair and relaxed. We had a dog named Lassie, a big shepherd dog. She would not bark at us or at anyone who came to visit us, but she would bark at something or someone that she had not seen coming to our place before. She started growling and barking. My wife said, "There is someone coming." Sure enough, even though it was very late, I heard footsteps in the snow, kind of squeaky like. Pretty soon, there was a knock on the door. I went and opened it and I had five visitors: John Fire Lame Deer, Richard Erdoes, and his wife and two sons.

My visitors had traveled to the Black Hills and had made several stops. They had car trouble coming back, but their intent was to see me before they left on their trip back to the Rosebud country. At that time, Richard Erdoes was in the process of writing a book.[7] I think the book's title is *'Lame Deer - Seeker of Vision'*. He made a tape, a short one. I spoke in that tape[8]. I do not recall what the tape said, but before he left, Richard reached in his pocket and gave me twenty dollars.

---

[7] The book referred to here is 'Lame Deer - Seeker of Vision' 1972 written and photographed by Richard Erdoes.

[8] The chapter in 'Lame Deer - Seeker of Vision' book, that was of Pete's taping that night was called, 'Talking to Owls and Butterflies.'

ON BEING A MEDICINE MAN

It is in a real out-of-time, out-of-the way manner that *Wakan Tanka* answers our prayers. I did not ask for help. All I said was "I want many more like this," meaning the place where I am, where it is the hardest, where the trials seem the hardest, where the problem is the heaviest, where tears usually come. That is the time the Great Spirit is closest, because He is always near us. I did not expect anything like this. Money was the farthest from my mind. But because of this, I know what my brother Joe said was true.

Once again, I would like to say a little bit about my home, the trailer camp. I doubt if anybody can live there in this kind of weather. It started to snow earlier this evening and the wind chill factor for the past week is down in the fifties, sixties, and seventies below zero. My home is one of these trailers that in the 1960s they hitched to a car and trailed along the highways. It is a narrow thing, and it is 30 feet long. But that is where I live. I am only glad to have a home.

This morning and yesterday morning, I went back there because I have a dog still living there and I had to feed it. I have my sweat lodge close by, all fenced up, with the wind blowing the covers away. But the sweat lodge rocks are there. The prayers of people, the prayers that I say are there; they echo from those very rocks. Those same rocks were red hot at one time, this past summer and the summer before. And it is there, part of a time period that *Wakan Tanka* was close to us, that He was close to us and helped us. And there, young men and young women have fasted at my sweat lodge. Some have used the sweat lodge, and some have gone out in

SACRED FIREPLACE

the country, out in the hills on *Hanbleceya* (Pipefast).

The place where I live is all hills; the terrain is rough. There are many ideal places where a person can *Hanbleceya*. That is where I live. I know that is where the good things will grow. If only we will see, even through the snow and the cold, the good things that *Wakan Tanka* has given us. Even though it is cold, even though there is snow, even though we suffer, even though we are hungry, even though our life seems in misery, far beyond that, He is always close by. In the depth of our troubles is the goodness of the Great Mystery. Always remember, that is the time to pray when the going is ruff because that is the time He is closest to you. And if you live as humbly as I do, you can be sure that the Great Spirit dwells there also.

Three (Yamni)

STORIES & LESSONS

Lakota Creation Story - "We Are Little Brother to the Buffalo"

I want to tell you how the buffalo and the Lakota became brothers. Long, long ago, so the legend goes, there was at that time, grass in the draws in these rolling plains that was above the waist. The grass was that tall, leaning over one way or the other. It was bountiful and wherever there was a herd of buffalo, there were always bulls. There was the head bull, and the younger ones. The bulls encircled the grazing buffalo herd because there would be calves among them, yearlings and smaller ones. In that time, there were bears and there were wolves plentiful on the plains. These bears and wolves would prey on the weak ones and the old buffalos. For protection, the leaders in the buffalo herd encircled the other buffalo and they would face out.

This legend tells us that an old buffalo bull was standing there on the plains. It was a cold and windy day. Somewhere, he heard a voice crying. The voice said four things: "I am cold. I am hungry. I am weak. I am thirsty." The old buffalo bull was listening. The power of the mysterious *Wakan Tanka* to instill into the mind of this old buffalo bull to think kindly is amazing. Besides, old bull was a fighter; he knew many years of battle with other bulls. He was a proud leader. But it is the work of the Great Spirit that He instilled into this buffalo the thought that what he was hearing, what he understood, was that someone was cold, hungry, weak, and thirsty. The buffalo bull sought the direction in which the voice was coming. But it was hard to discern because the wind was blowing. He would go down close to the earth, and he would try to follow the sound, that weeping, that crying.

In the course of time, he came to a blood clot. It was this blood clot that was crying, "I am cold. I am hungry. I am weak. I am thirsty." The old buffalo bull sniffed at it and he looked very closely. That blood clot was the Lakota people, the Red Man. It was there that the Great Mystery inspired in this buffalo that he would give everything of himself, his whole being, even his spirit, to this one in need.

So, the buffalo bull said to this crying individual, "I will be your big brother. I will give you all that I am. Look at me, I am strong. I am not weak, I am strong. I went through all these years fighting my battles, winning out. I bear the scars of battle. But I am victorious and I am to this point in life, a leader in the herd so I am not weak. Look about you. All over creation is my feed. I can eat here. I can eat there. I can eat everywhere so I am never hungry. Look at me.

"Look at me. Look at my mane. The forepart of my being is all fur. When the blizzard winds blow, I walk facing the blowing wind and can eat the grass on the way. And when I stand still, I face the wind because the forepart of my being is all fur and I am never cold. So, I will make you my little brother. We will be like one; we will be together. You can have my hide to live in. You can have my flesh to eat so you will not be hungry. You will be like me. When you do these things, you will be strong."

So there at that instant, that moment, the buffalo and the Lakota became brothers. That is why the Lakota use every part of the buffalo that they kill. Not one single part of it is wasted or thrown away. In many instances, the Lakota used buffalo for a curing of any sickness. That part of the meat on the hump of the buffalo is held sacred by the Lakota. We use that mixed with medicine.

If this world continued in the fashion before the white man came, we would still be a lovely beautiful people. There would be buffalo on the land. There would be deer and all kinds of animals, along with the Lakota people.

They call it the "Wild, Wild West." It was paradise before the white man. It was only wild after the white man came, because they shot at random, at anything that moved. They did away with the buffalo and with all the wild game; only a few

SACRED FIREPLACE

animals remain. The buffalo that we know are in the state parks and just recently, some people have buffalo ranches. That is the greed of the white man. What the Creator made in this Western Hemisphere was meant for the Native people but the white man came and took it all.

Long before the advent of the white man with his medical profession and medical techniques reached the Indian country, we as Lakota people have performed blood transfusions. When the warriors would go out on a hunt, they would bring back buffalo blood. If there was a very sick person who was just hide and bones, the medicine man would give that person a drink of buffalo blood. The medicine man would take a spoonful of the buffalo's live blood, the warm live blood, and give it to the sick.

Three years ago, on the Standing Rock Reservation where we used to conduct the Sundances, they were butchering a buffalo and I asked to go along. My son, Peter Catches, came along too. I purposely took a cup with me. When they started butchering, when they had it open, I reached under the *taniga* (tripe) and got a cupful of buffalo blood and I drank it. Everybody was startled. They really looked at me. Peter came over and said, "Dad, get me some." So, when I drank it up I reached over, got a cupful and handed it to him. He drank it, too. This is what the Native Americans did long ago. Now we see this as a blood transfusion. When the buffalo gave his all to the Lakota people, that is what he meant. He is life giving. The buffalo gave everything of himself to his younger brother so that he can be strong, so that he can continue to live in this world.

STORIES & LESSONS

WINTER COUNT

In the books that you read about our people, the Lakota, we are always referred to as savages. The books say of us that we are pagan worshippers, and that we are heathens. But from the beginning of time, we have always been inspired by the Great Mystery, as it is with our people even today. We have to search to find out why we are here in this world. I will now touch on a tale of long ago. It has to do with a buffalo hunt, a warrior, and his hunting pony.

Our people are nomadic; we traveled around the *Ka Sapa* (Black Hills). Being that the buffalo sacrifices his whole life to help his younger brother, the Lakota, the Lakota people stayed close to buffalo herds. Buffalo numbered in millions and millions. You did not have to look for them. All you

SACRED FIREPLACE

had to do was go over the hill and you could run into a bunch.

Throughout the summer, the warriors took care of their hunting ponies. They even bathed them. Sometimes, the horse bathed itself. They would take them to the creek wherever they are camped and let them stand in the water. While standing up, the horses would splash the water with their foreleg. They would lay down and sometimes half roll over. They would get up, paw the water and then lay down on the other side. But generally, a warrior that loves his pony will do this bathing for him. The pony understands this and stands still. The warrior would take a container, dip water, standing beside his horse in midstream and splash water on the horse, including the tail, the mane, the underside, everywhere. He takes real good care of him.

This standing in the water and staying there for quite a while serves a dual purpose. It gives the horse time to soften its hooves so they can grow out a little more. By fall, it will be like this horse is shod with horseshoes. The horse can run or turn, and even make a U-turn and not fall down, scraping the ice with that screeching sound. These ponies are surefooted.

So, this warrior took care of his pony all summer, fed him good, took him out to a good place with plenty of feed and staked him out. They began to understand each other. The warrior would sit on top of a hill and watch him. They would talk. The warrior would talk to his horse. In doing this, the horse and rider then understood each other. They came to love each another.

STORIES & LESSONS

The Lakota settled down for winter encampment along a river. Most generally, the camp was along the Missouri River. They had to select a place where there was an abundance of dry wood and that was close to a river so they could get their water. It was not always in one place. They had to change year after year. They would select a place with a windbreak. Of course, they had to look after their horses.

Even when they are at winter camp, stationary for the whole of winter, there came a time when the people had to have fresh meat. It could have been because of a special occasion, or because of sickness in the camp. But whatever the reason, a buffalo hunt was required in the winter. It had to be done.

This particular hunt happened to be on a day when there was a blizzard. The warriors, being accustomed to the many various elements, used different ways to protect themselves. On a day such as this, they would wear a buffalo robe wrapped around their body with a strip of rawhide to tie at the belt. Beneath this buffalo robe from the waist up was what you might call a deerskin shirt or jacket with fringe sleeves, back, and skirting.

For this buffalo hunt, a particular warrior painted his face and his horse, too. He painted the horse's legs with signs of his dreams. He did this to invoke the Great Spirit to help this horse and its rider on this special buffalo hunt.

The band of warriors came upon a herd of buffalo on this near blizzard day. This warrior and his horse singled out a buffalo and chased it. Because of the blizzard, vision was sometimes next to nothing and

SACRED FIREPLACE

the singled out buffalo turned away from the main herd. The rest of the hunters took after the main herd but this warrior was chasing the lone buffalo.

For this warrior and his horse, this would not be the first kill of the day. Perhaps it was the second one. But he had to have two or three. He was thinking of those at camp who were hungry for fresh meat - the children, the elderly, the blind, the sick, the orphaned, the widowed, the unfortunate. That is why he invoked the Great Spirit to help him get two or three buffalos. He was on the crest of a hill and it was very cold. Because it had probably rained before the storm, it was icy.

As the storm cleared a little, he saw what looked like a stand of snakeweed at a distance. The buffalo was running towards it. Just as the warrior was about to get next to the buffalo to begin to shed his outer buffalo robe, take his bow and arrow, and put an arrow into the buffalo, some instinct told him that he must turn aside. His pony was well shod; its hooves were grown out and the horse made a u-turn, shedding ice and making a screeching sound. His horse went skidding on the ice and turned from the edge of that huge cliff just in time and the buffalo went over. How can a savage, how can a pagan worshipper, who knew that he was just about to kill his second or third buffalo, and the need was great, why would he turn from it? What looked to be a bunch of snakeweed was in reality the tip of huge cottonwood trees down at the base of the cliff. The buffalo that went over that embankment got caught halfway down in the huge crutch of one of the cottonwood trees.

STORIES & LESSONS

It seemed to the Lakota warrior that it was a sacrifice, that no man nor beast would get to that meat. A sacrifice is to the Indian something that you offer to the Great Spirit and **to the Great Spirit alone**. Because the buffalo was caught halfway up that bank, no man could get to it, although wolves, coyotes, bear, and wildcats could.

Long after the spring, the people came to that place to check on it; and what remained of that buffalo was a shrunken skeleton. And those that could come to the buffalo did not, because it was an offering to the Great Spirit, and meant for the Great Spirit alone.

This story has been told from generation to generation. It was part of what is known as the winter count. The winter count is drawings of events, like a calendar for each year. It is done on a stretched out, dry buffalo hide. It was scraped clean and made pliable. The reason why they call it a winter count is that most of the paintings on that buffalo hide are events of the winter, such as a great famine, or a great sickness that perhaps wiped out part of the tribe. Events were painted on the buffalo hide each year. They started from the center and went clockwise, coming to a full circle and starting again. This kept going until it reached the outer edges of the buffalo robe.

I remember the winter count of the year I was born, which is 1912. In our language, that winter-count was "When the White Cat Came to Our Camp," *Igmu Ska Wan He*.

That is the story of a buffalo hunt, a warrior, and his pony - a story lovable and beautiful because the Great Spirit's hand was in it. The Great Spirit meant that buffalo to be offered to Him because this was a special, excellent warrior and his horse. That warrior could have had that buffalo. But, since it was caught in the crutch of this huge cottonwood tree, the people looked at it as an offering to the Great Spirit, and it became a winter count event, a story to be remembered.

So, you see, man and horse functioned as one, in unison, to make life pleasant for themselves and for the people. There are songs about the wind, the streams, the mountains, the day, the night, the dawn of a new day. There are songs that pertain to the seasons of the year. And, there are songs of our people about the horse and the buffalo too.

THE DEITY OF THE BRAVE

by *Zintkala Oyate*

This is a recollection of a sacred dream, as it was recounted to me. It has been necessary to carefully translate the original oral account, because of the distinct language differences found between the Lakota and English languages. I have undertaken this task to the best of my ability.

Liquid fire splashes across the sky; the earth trembles from the roar of a thousand Thunder Beings. The circle of teepees surrounds the main fire in the center; and an opening ten lodge lengths wide faces the east.

The landscape towards the east is a shallow meadow, with a small brook flowing through the

STORIES & LESSONS

high underbrush. The hills above the brook are covered with a blanket of pine, so natural to this environment. In the meadow is the herd of stallions that belongs to the encampment, the encampment is that of the Lakota *Oyate*.

West of the encampment lies the prairie, with its sea of natural grass as high as a man's waist. Nearer to the encampment is a lone hill, a lone breast coming out of Mother Earth. There a shadowed figure is seen walking, walking slowly in a manner none can understand.

Around the main fire inside of the encampment, stand the dog warriors, who were the night guard. They have come in, having been replaced by the day guard. Some of the people of the village are now beginning to move about. It is dawn.

Flashes of light blind those who look up. A shaking of the earth and a crashing noise wake those who still sleep. The stallions in the meadow are restlessly milling about, as if wondering if some unseen fury may be about to descend upon them. The shadowy figure slowly continues to walk up the lone hill. He is unmindful of the eyes that still watch him from the camp. The voices of the people are muffled; their hands are pointed; their unswerving attention is attracted to this lone figure, as he slowly continues to walk in a way none had ever seen before.

In the meadow, the air is thick and still, and then there is a flash of lightning with a thunderclap of a kind that one will hear once in a lifetime. The earth quakes enough to chill the blood. The consciousness of the camp, the Lakota *Oyate*, knows this pattern for they have seen and felt such things

SACRED FIREPLACE

at other times. They know that the loving hand of the Great Spirit is about to touch one of His children.

From the meadow there comes a loud neighing and, from among the milling herd, there darts forth a horse like no other. Huge in stature, it is as if three horses had become one, yet this horse controls its rhythm as only a deer would. It jumps, darts, and kicks in the air as if crazed.

The figure can now be seen at the very top of the hill with his arms outstretched toward the heavens. Lightning seems to be touching his hands at every flash and at each resounding, echoing clap of thunder. The horse seems responsible for the shaking of the earth, as it gallops wildly towards the lone figure still standing with his arms outstretched towards the heavens.

The dog warriors and the awakened people watch in wonder and in amazement. It seems as though everything is now occurring in slow motion. The big drops of rain can be distinctly seen as they slowly fall. Each person's next heartbeat seems to be an eternity away. Everyone can feel themselves breathing each molecule of air, one at a time.

The maddened horse has turned and suddenly reaches the camp. Everyone is alarmed, and yet nothing is done, for nothing can be done. Now the *Oyate* see that this horse is foaming at the mouth. The horse has been dancing, bucking, jumping, and rearing up. Again it turns towards the hill, the lone hill towards the west, and rears up for the last time. It takes off at a full gallop in the direction of the hill, where the lone figure still stands with outstretched hands towards the heavens.

STORIES & LESSONS

The main medicine man in the encampment of the Lakota *Oyate* gathers about him the sacred drum singers, for they know the songs, the songs of the people, the first people of peace. They know the songs of birth, of living life, and of death itself. He moves slowly, deliberately, with the full measure of wisdom befitting one who has been chosen to be above other holy men. His station was ordained by destiny, just as was the Mother, our Earth, destined to travel around the sun. Some portions of one's life are simply a part of a greater purpose.

He is old. Life has stamped the creases of myriad lines upon his face. They have been beautifully carved, moment by moment, by the fingers of time's emotions; and behind this inscription there lingers quietly the wisdom of the ages, handed down from generation to generation in experiential teachings. He too had visions. He too had psychic dreams. He too had inclinations. And he had possessed, in all of his years, the ability to relive such moments again and again. He knew very well of this perfection; it had become a symbiotic part of him. The Great Mystery had revealed these moments to him and now he is prepared. He will do his part and he will do it well.

The frenzied horse is a dappled gray. It is a magnificent creature. Lucidly flowing, it slowly rushes in a dreamlike gallop; its color is a faint sky blue in the awakening dawn. This holy man had seen this reality before; and now how frighteningly wonderful it is to be a part of this mystery. He remembers the before and the after; and now, he hears the living, the crying - the crying he had heard many times.

SACRED FIREPLACE

In the quietness of the meadow, in the stillness of the cool crisp air, a dear and resounding voice can be heard. It is a voice in the beginning of this chant:

Tunkasila wa mung yanka yo
Le miyaca nawajin yelo
Wa mung yanka yo
Le miyaca nawajin yelo

Tunkasila wa mung yanka yo
Le miyaca nawajin yelo
Wa mung yanka yo
Le miyaca nawajin yelo

Grandfathers look at me
This is I that is standing
Look at me
This is I that is standing

The echoing chant reverberates in the meadow, which is quiet no longer. The sacred drum singers beat the drum in rhythmic unison and the sound of the gushing chant becomes a song of vision.

The shadowed lone figure is no longer alone. The horse and the man have become absorbed into one; they have become one spirit. This man, this warrior is personified, and has become a link between the material physical world and the beyond of the spiritual world.

STORIES & LESSONS

That old wrinkled medicine man of so many years had already known that this part of the vision was to be a reality. And he is quiet as he sits now in the dark serene silence of the *inipi*. He hears the guttural voices no longer. The visions are gone and there to his right at the back of the lodge sits the warrior. He knows what this warrior must do in the years to come. It will be his destiny to live the visions and to make them into reality upon this earth. He knows that this warrior is special, that he is the epitome of the brave, the Deity of the Brave.

SACRED FIREPLACE

Near the spot the buffalo laid in the legend

THE LEGEND OF "PTE WOKU"
by Zinktala Oyate

This is how this legend was told to me by Petaga Yuha Mani (He Walks with Hot Coals). He, in turn, was told this legend by Alfred Ribsman, a survivor of Wounded Knee massacre, who was my maternal grandfather.

This valley where we have the annual *Pte Woku* (Feeding of the Buffalo) Sundance was once known as Red Feather Valley. This valley is now a part of the Calico Community and it is known as a very special place. The valley is a place of such spiritual

STORIES & LESSONS

presence that many people go there to do their fasts. My father did his first and most personal Sundance there in the summer of 1964, and for the past thirty-six years, I have conducted the Spotted Eagle Sundance in this valley. One of its stories which took place in this valley is about a young man in his late twenties or early thirties who had done a *Hanbleceya* (Pipefast) in a certain area where there is a high butte, which can be seen from a few miles away. It is generally called Mission Butte, because the Catholic mission school was nearby.

This young man's fast took place in the early 1920s. The exact location of his *Hanbleceya* was right on top of that butte. He was to fast for four days and four nights, but on the second morning when the medicine man watching over him went there to check up on him, the young man was gone. There were no tracks on the soft earth, no disturbances of any kind indicating that he left the area where he had been designated to pray to the Great Mystery.

Those were the horse-and-buggy days and there were no means of fast communication. So, his family sent out runners on horseback to nearby towns, even to other states and to other tribes, to see if anyone of that description had been seen passing through the area. No one had even so much as heard of him, let alone seen him. The story goes that being a good soul, he had simply gone from that hilltop right into the Land of the Winds (heaven).

Another legend about this place occurred in the 1830s. The *Lakota Oyate* were camped nearby in

SACRED FIREPLACE

the springtime of the year. Because it was spring, the food supply was low, and the people were hungry. Warriors were sent out from the encampment to see if they could get some small game since there were no buffalo herds close by. Scout warriors were sent out in every direction.

When one warrior came upon Red Feather Valley, he decided to explore the entire area. As midday approached, he climbed a hill that had a long ridge covered with pines. Once on top, he sat down on the ground in the shade of one of the large conifers that overlooked the valley. Since it was midday, he decided to have his meal of *papa* (dried meat), and drink some water from his bladder container.

The long ridged hill where he rested stands north of our Sundance grounds of today. As he sat there resting and eating in the coolness of the shade, he gazed about and noticed the beauty of the place. Then he noticed something different, something out of place, on the other side of the valley. From where the warrior sat, he had a clear view down a steep incline to a creek bottom. The creek is fed by natural springs which are farther up the valley. On the other side of the creek bottom, which is thick with ash, elm, and other trees and shrubs indigenous to the area, there is another steep sloping hill, which rises up to a large flat area. This flat area is where the warrior had seen something unusual. Something had stirred inside of him. He felt strange emotions unlike the natural highs and lows one might feel on any ordinary day.

He felt a deep apprehension, and he needed to know what had stirred those feelings inside of him. He arose, went down the ridge and crossed the creek. He deliberately and slowly made his way up the hill leading to the flat area. As he cautiously peered over onto the flat area, he noticed that at its back, near the tree line and somewhat to the east, there was a buffalo lying down. His first thought was to retrieve an arrow and thread it to his bowstring, which he did.

But as he continued to watch, he came to the conclusion that the buffalo was already dead. He put the arrow back into his quiver, shouldered his bow, and slowly approached the huge bison. By the looks of it, he thought it must be a three year-old bull. But he was not sure and needed to take a closer look.

As he came up to it, he noticed that the bison bull was breathing, but that its breaths were very shallow. He moved closer still and put his ear to its neck, by its throat. He could hear the faintest slow beat of its heart. His next thoughts were confused. "Why is this lone buffalo here? Why is he not near the cool streams where there is shade and the tender sprouts of new grass? Did the Great Mystery put this bull here for me to kill and take back to the people? Why is it that I feel that it is meant to live, and that I am to nurse it back to life?"

Being a Lakota, he understood that the bison and his nation were brothers and he decided to go with the last thought. He felt reinforced by the extraordinary nature of this situation. He was uplifted by his affirmation and was sure that the Great Mystery approved of his decision.

With that he went down to the stream and filled up his bladder container. He cut two heaping armfuls of the fresh grass and went back up to

SACRED FIREPLACE

where the buffalo lay. With deliberate earnestness, he petted and talked to his brother. "Take this food and eat it. It is medicine. Take this water and drink it. It is medicine." As their eyes met, an understanding was made and the buffalo ate some grass and drank some water, even though, as the warrior noticed, it took just a little. Nevertheless, he knew through experience that the healing had started.

He stayed there for a time, and in the evening, he started back to his camp but not before telling his brother that he would take care of him until he got well, and not to be afraid, for he would be watching over him. With that, he started back to his camp.

On the way back to camp, he felt that he had done the right thing about that day's happening. Yet, at the same time he felt empty, because he was sent out to find food and he was bringing nothing back. He had nothing to show for his day's hunt. As the warrior approached the encampment of his people, he heard drums. He heard the shouts and yells of happiness. His spirit soared as he entered the circle of the village and discovered that all of the other warriors had been very successful, that a big celebration was underway.

The people were happy and milled around a huge bonfire as each warrior took a turn relating what he had encountered in that day. The people listened with enthusiastic imaginations and yelled whoops of approval and agreement, verifying that they would have done the same as the warriors had they been in their place.

Now, it came to the turn of the warrior who had gone to the Red Feather Valley to talk about his

STORIES & LESSONS

day and tell what had happened during his hunt. The scout warrior stood up and the people, realizing that this was the one warrior who came back empty-handed, listened with great curiosity to his story.

After he had completed his tale, he described the location where the bison bull laid. He asked if he had made a right decision. There was a great deal of conversation then and finally one of the spiritual elders stood up and said, "Human emotion cannot be denied. Spiritual matters are a factor in the development of understanding. Reason is a part of the creative force of all things in the Holy Swirl of the universe. Why is that buffalo there, alone and separated from his herd, sick, hungry and dying? It is this warrior's honor of obligation to do the things he said to the buffalo and, later on, if the Great Mystery, the All Knowing, shows us why this is so, then that too is good! The entire camp will stay at this spot until there is a change."

With all approving, the elder silently sat down. Then the warrior stood up and told everyone to stay away from that particular area. The celebration continued till dawn.

For the next week and into the following week, the warrior fed and brought cool water to drink to his brother. Then one morning, while he watched, the bison began to struggle. First he got onto his knees, then onto one leg. Then he fought his way up to two legs, and finally he was standing. The warrior's bison brother was still very weak and staggered about as he walked and yet, the warrior felt that rush of joy, sensed the continuation of the miracle of life under even these bleak circumstances. He was very happy and tears welled up in his eyes as he saw the look and expression of acknowledgment in his brother's gaze.

The warrior began to look forward to spending time with his brother every morning. He noticed that with each passing day, the bison got stronger and pawed more and more at the earth with it, his hooves and dug even more energetically with his horns. In the evenings, you could hear the bellowing of his bison brother for miles.

One morning the scout warrior found that his spirit brother was gone. His immediate reaction was of panic and alarm. He searched the whole area to no avail. He knew now that his spirit brother had gone back to his own people and he felt very sad at this loss. He took his sadness back to the encampment with him. He took it to the medicine man and, with a heavy heart, told of the things he felt, of the bond that was made between his spirit brother and him. The medicine man sat in silence for a while and then he said, "That bond will always be there, in its time, where it belongs. You must cherish those moments and, in some way, they will help you to understand and to continue on."

The whole camp prepared to move to another location when they heard that the buffalo had gotten well. In that particular division of the nation, it is said that year was known as "the year when the buffalo got well." Many years passed, perhaps eighteen or nineteen, when this particular encampment found itself isolated in the Badlands, in what is now South Dakota. They were caught there in a huge snowstorm, a real blizzard. Their food supply was nearly gone and so they sent out

STORIES & LESSONS

scout warriors to hunt but the buffalo's brother was not included among them. He was now old and weak and it was feared that he might die in the icy cold of the blinding storm.

But the buffalo's brother was not pleased to be left behind. He went to the village's *naca* (leader) and pleaded with him. He explained that all of his life he had toiled for the benefit of others. He stated that he was a servant of the people. He declared that within his heart—a warrior's heart—he knew that if he should die in the storm, striving to protect the people, he would die willingly, as was the way of his spirit. The *naca* let him go.

Back in his lodge, he spoke solemnly to his wife. "Be strong, and if I don't come back, do not worry, we will see each other again." With that, he left. As he left the sheltered windbreak of the teepees, he could only see a few feet in front of his face. There was blinding whiteness everywhere he looked so he decided to go with the wind, for that would save his energy. That night he slept in a crevice.

In the morning he got up and jumped around to circulate his blood. The storm was raging as the day before and he continued until he ran right into something. It had fur and was warm and the old warrior was excited but he was also weak from the icy cold which engulfed him. To his surprise, the bull laid down with his back to the wind. So the old warrior laid right down next to him, up against the belly of that old bull and became warm.

After a time, the old bull started to move and get up onto his feet. Upon standing, it seemed as if he was waiting for something. So the old warrior got up and started to feel the old bull. That power or essence known to us as *nagi* (spirit) flowed gently and there was recognition as the bull bellowed several times. At that moment, the old warrior really knew. The bull now was also old and yet he was huge. He started to walk slowly away from the old warrior and stopped as if to wait. The warrior knew then what to do and he grabbed hold of the bull's tail and followed behind him until it grew dark. Then the old buffalo laid down as before and the old warrior warmed up again, laying against the belly of his spirit brother.

When they started up again the next day, the blizzard was worse than before. They traveled slowly until the old bull finally stopped and laid down. The old warrior scout began to really understand what was going on when he realized that he was back at the encampment of his people. He yelled out a loud *akisa* (war whoop) and the people came running to where he stood. When he turned around to look at his brother who still laid there, he saw that the spark of life was gone. In this legend, we find that the warrior and the bison bull had come full circle in each other in order to fulfill a greater purpose in life.

STORIES & LESSONS

Petaga Yuha Mani in traditional home (teepee) with altar in foreground

TRUTH AND HONESTY

In my early life I went to a Jesuit school where one of the concepts that makes up the religion is to never lie. The missionary, who taught religious

SACRED FIREPLACE

instruction in a catechism class, stressed the fact that truth and honesty are the best means of living a good life. He emphasized his instructions by telling stories.

The missionary said we must be very careful, extra careful, of how we live in this world—even to the point of what one red penny could do. One red penny is nearly worthless by itself but ninety-nine others make one dollar. If someone kept a penny meant for the people, that would hinder that person's entry into heaven. So, he stressed the fact that honesty is the most vital part of any person serving in the capacity that serves the public.

I often recall those stories I heard as a young man; they mean so much to me. Although I do not follow this Jesuit religion anymore, I know that some of the values we were taught are good. One of the things I want to make clear is that I do not claim to know it all. As human beings, we all make mistakes. I think it is these stories that kept me from going too much into the bad way of life. And as a human being, I, too, have my faults. I am impatient at times and I get angry at times. It is like this with the tribal government and the many areas and departments that serve the people. The people who serve in those departments are human beings and they like to play favorites and they like to be underhanded sometimes. I do not claim that I am not that way. I try hard not to be. Again, I will say I am not perfect. I am saying that I am not the judge. I am not saying that all the rest of the world is no good. There are good people in the world; there is good in all peoples.

STORIES & LESSONS

Honesty is one of the things that is essential. It is very, very important that we be honest, not only with others, but most especially with ourselves. We must be honest with ourselves, and that way, if it comes from within us, then we know we can be honest with everyone around us that we come in contact with.

Honesty to me is so great a value that all people should make it a custom as long as we are in this world. It is one of the foundations that could bring about peace. Even a powerful nation like the United States is sometimes lacking in honesty. The United States government, if it was honest, would uphold the treaties that it made with Native Americans.

I will tell you a tale about honesty. I will not mention names. This man is related to us, people know him; people living now know him. In his days he was a warrior, a clean honest warrior. This was in the fall of the year back in the covered wagon days. There was an encampment of Indian people and this young warrior was a part of that camp. The warriors, known as dog soldiers, did all the work of a camp. They were also known as the *Tokala* (fox) society. They kept the main fire going throughout the day and night so that if one of the smaller fires elsewhere in the camp went out, the people would take the main fire in the center and start their fire again. The *Tokala* society had a big job to do. They took care of the elderly and the sick, and after a hunt, they brought back the buffalo meat to those in need - the orphans, the old, the weak, the sick, and the widowed.

Throughout our history, kept in oral history, the Indian people have taken care of their own needs

SACRED FIREPLACE

because this is a way of life that was fashioned by the Great Spirit and infused in the hearts and minds of the Indian people. Our name, Lakota, means "Peace." We are a peaceful people. Only when our hunting area was invaded did we act to protect ourselves.

But like anywhere else and in any organization, there is bound to be some group that tries to bring disharmony. One fall night, some young men in the camp got together and sneaked off to waylay a covered-wagon train. In a fight such as this, they might take the oxen or the horses that drew the wagons in order to stop the wagon train and then let the people go or they might choose to handle the situation according to their plan of warfare. This night, the young men stopped a wagon and they killed the men, women, and everyone else who were a part of that wagon train. The only exception was one young girl. They set fire to everything, killed the team of horses, and took captive this one white girl.

At the time the policy of an Indian encampment was that when they took someone prisoner, the matter would have to be taken before the "council fire." They would have a council in the evening with a bonfire burning. At the council fire, people that have any attachment to the issue at hand were given time to talk.

So, this white girl was taken before the council fire. Those who captured her and brought her back explained the situation. This honest warrior was sitting there listening to what was being said. In the ensuing talk about what to do with the white girl, the honest warrior stood up and told the council that he is married to a good woman and his intentions are not upon another woman. He stated that what he had was what he wanted and he did not want anything more. He then told the white girl's story in such a way that people listened real closely.

"This white girl's parents, uncles or aunts, or whomever, have been wiped away, so this white girl is grieving. She is in sorrow. I want this white girl to live in my home and my wife will take care of her. We will give her the choicest of meat to eat, give her a place of honor with many buffalo hides to sleep on and keep her warm through the winter months. In the spring, when the ponies are fed and grow fat and lively, when new life is born in the ponies, I will select two honest warriors to go with me to take this white girl to the nearest army post."

The chiefs that were in charge of this council fire decided that this was the best they had heard and they gave this honest warrior the white girl to care for. He took her back to his camp and explained to his wife that she was in charge of her and that she was to feed her first because she was an honored guest. The wife was to give her the best of the meat and when she drew fresh water, to give her the first drink. Lastly, the wife should go with the girl to the bathroom or wherever she went and watch over her so she would not be afraid.

Because of the warrior's intent and preparation, the white girl was well taken care of through the winter months. Her grieving for her lost relatives soon faded away - time heals all pain and time heals all sorrow. She was taught to learn the sign language. In midwinter, she could be heard to laugh

SACRED FIREPLACE

and she began to understand the language that we speak.

The winter months quickly passed and spring came upon the Indian encampment. Ice melted in the streams. Greening began to show itself—green grass and buds on the trees. Ponies were cropping the green grass and began to grow fat. As was the custom of the time, scouts were sent out. The honest warrior told the scouts to see where the closest army post was located. They scouted the countryside and along a big river and soon came upon a fort. Distances were gauged by the travel during a day, and the scouts estimated that it was a three-day ride to the army post. They brought back the news to this virtuous warrior.

The warrior selected two honest, straightforward warriors to go with him to take the white girl to the army post. They traveled slowly and on the third day, they came upon the army post. It was the custom at that time, when you were on horseback, that when you come upon the horizon, you would turn sideways for them to see you. You would then turn the other way, and show your flag of truce, an indication that they could talk or parley. If the people in the fort accepted the parley, they would signal from the fort by opening the big gates. So, when the three warriors came upon that horizon overlooking the fort, they showed themselves by turning the horses sideways. Through their field glasses, the solders saw three Indian warriors and one white girl and so they threw open the fort gates. The warriors walked their horses slowly. When they entered the fort, the infantry was all lined up with the cavalry behind them and the army commanders were standing near the flagpole.

STORIES & LESSONS

The Indians rode to the center. This white girl jumped off her horse, ran to the captain, pointed to the honest warriors and said, "They raped me. I was captured in the fall and they treated me mean all through the winter." So, instead of respect for the good deed they had done, they were imprisoned. They were put in irons and thrown into a cell. The army post commanders had a meeting to see what they should do with the three warriors. After days of searching for a solution, they finally agreed to kill them. The general went to see the prisoners and told them, "When the sun comes up, we will take you three on horseback out that way. There is a hill, a long hill. We will go up on that hill and go to the very end to a point over there and shoot you." He said this, but he used motions so that the Indians would understand. This honest warrior agreed to what was being communicated.

Throughout the time the warriors were imprisoned, a ball and chain was fastened to their ankles. That same chain came up and was fastened around their wrists. It was awkward and made of heavy iron so it cut into their flesh. The least movement they made was painful and irritating.

The next morning the soldiers fed them good and the warriors were readied and mounted. Through the night, the honest warrior was telling the others, "I will give one word and that word is "*hokahey*." Every Indian, even today, knows what that word means. "When I holler "*hokahey*," we will go full speed ahead to one side, to your right."

Only one horse had a lead rope to one soldier. The rest were tied together. From the first horse

SACRED FIREPLACE

and rider, the lead rope was tied to the second, and from the second horse, the lead rope was tied to the third rider's horse. The Indian and solders rode to that long hill and knew when they had arrived. The Indians could talk with their eyes. When they were coming to that point to where they were going to be shot, this honest warrior turned his head. That little movement told the others to be ready. He hollered, "*Hokahey!*" The horses, as one, went forward so quickly and so powerfully that the lead rope that was held by the soldier came away. The warriors and their horses went down that hill running all out. The soldiers were so taken by surprise that they could not get their pistols out and by the time the warriors were shot at, they were out of rifle range.

There were big bushes and sagebrush everywhere - it must have been in Wyoming country. The warriors had to jump or go around the brush but they were all running smoothly; none of them tripped, although they were still tied together. The Indian ponies at that time were used to buffalo hunts and running like that. You had to use your knees to guide them and they would obey. It is said ,that at that time, the Indian rider and his horse were like one machine working in harmony to perfection. There was no need for a whip. Just a holler of "*hokahey*," and his horse would give all that he had.

The previous night there must have been a downpour in that region because they came upon a swollen river and stopped at the bank. This honest warrior, held up his hands and said, "Great Spirit, help us through this stream. If you help us escape, I will dance the Sundance next summer."

STORIES & LESSONS

Just think what we do today, in comparison to the times this story took place. The honest warrior said next summer, not this summer. If it was us doing that, we would most likely say this summer. But traditionally, a ceremony such as the Sundance or the Pipefast required one year of preparation. They had to prepare to have their Pipe in order and the essential parts to make up their regalia. And most of all, they had to prepare their inside. If they are easy to anger, they should quit that; they should throw that away. Try hard not to get angry. If they are not honest, they should go all out trying to be honest, because when they approach that sacred place, they will go in the presence of the Great Spirit. If they have impure things inside of them, such as dishonesty, unkindness, being quarrelsome and other such things, the Great Spirit will not be at that sacred place.

So this honest warrior reached out his hand and said, "Great Spirit, help me. Help us through this stream. Help us escape and I will dance the Sundance next year, next summer." Summer was just two or three months away, but he meant the next summer, for he needed preparation time to be ready.

They say that the warriors and their ponies trotted through that flood and the water went just above the knees of the horses that they rode. The pursuing soldiers, seeing this, rushed head on into that stream. It was deep, so when they rushed in there, they fell into the deep water. One horse was drowned and its rider nearly drowned too. How is it that these three Indians, when they passed through the stream, it was just shallow, just above the knees of the horses, and when the soldiers came, it was a deep raging flood where a horse drowned?

The story goes on to say that, after their escape, the honest warrior prepared himself from that summer through the ensuing months, through the following winter, and on into the next summer. By the time the next summer came, he was ready. He pierced on both sides of his chest the first day and he danced, fighting the rawhide thongs that were tied to the Sundance Tree for four days, sometimes just falling from sheer exhaustion. But he fulfilled his promise to the Great Spirit that, if they escaped from the pursuing soldiers, he would dance the Sun-dance.

The warrior fulfilled his promise, and he related his story in the years after. His wrists and ankles were scarred from the ball and chains for the remainder of his life, in testimony of an honest warrior who would go far to do a good deed for one of his fellow human beings. Before he passed from this world, he said, "My wrists and my ankles bear the scars of honesty. You can be scarred by being honest but the Great Spirit loves you all the more because of your honesty."

THE STORY OF BLAH BLAH

by *Zintkala Oyate*

In our country, the Seven Sacred Rites are cherished in our hearts.

STORIES & LESSONS

There was once a simple man. He always came and helped prepare when it was time for the purification rite. He would fix the rocks, pick new sage and put it inside; build the fire and watch over it, acted as the doorman and brought in the stones (grandfathers), and he would wait while the others had their ceremony. When it was over, he would wait around to hear when they would hold the next purification rite, and then he would leave. Upon doing so, he gathered new sage and collected new stones and would sweep and clean everything up in preparation for the next purification rite. He was the medicine man's brother-in-law, the medicine man's wife's brother. They made fun of him because he was a simple man. They called him Blah Blah. In our country, that's not a good way in which to refer to another person. He didn't care. He was a simple man. He enjoyed what he was doing because he loved the Great Mystery. He knew he was accomplishing something the others couldn't. They were busy going about their lives.

Well, it so happened one day they had a purification rite (sweat lodge) and afterward they asked him, "Hey, Blah Blah, do you ever think about going up on the hill?" We sometimes call the Pipefast as going on the hill. He said, "Yea, yea, I did. I have." Right away they started looking at each other with big smiles. "We'll put you up." The simple man said, "I don't have nothing. All I have is what you see before you. That's why I do these things for you because that's all I can do." Right away they looked at each other. One said, "My wife will make you some moccasins." The other said, "My wife will make you a star quilt." The other one said, "I'll furnish the buffalo skull." The other one

SACRED FIREPLACE

said, "We'll make you the tobacco ties; we'll get everything ready for you."

Blah Blah grew really big right then. He was the happiest person in the world. Nothing could have come close to this in his life for this was a miracle. All the time the other ones were making fun of him. They said, "Next weekend" which was the middle of July, they were going to put him up. He said, "Yea, ok, I'm ready." So they prepared him. There was one place that everyone stayed away from for their Pipefast. They were afraid of this place. It was a high hill, surrounded by other high hills, perhaps a danger zone. So they decided to put him up there. His sister was against it but she couldn't go against the medicine man. So everything was prepared. He went into the purification rite, got everything ready and they took him. They had to go through a dry creek bed, up and over a big old hill and around a corner. There was a spot that was a flat area and they put him there. They all sang songs. It was a bright hot day. They set up his area, put the cherry trees up, put his tobacco ties up, his alter, and everything. He had his Pipe that one of his cousins had made for him. He was all set, he was happy. He was happy to go in front of the Great Mystery. So they all said, "Pray out loud." And so he started praying before they even left. One of them said, "If you want to, you can even cry." They all started leaving single file and there he was, crying. One of them said to the medicine man, "Look at him, he's crying." The medicine man looked at him and said, "That's because you told him to cry."

So back down the hill they went. That night they had a ceremony in support of him. They called it a singing. Everybody was there. All were happy to see that finally somebody cared enough to put him up on the hill. They prepared food in support and they all prayed. The medicine man put his alter up and they went into ceremony in support. Suddenly, a big storm came from out of nowhere. Lightning was flashing and big chunks of hail were falling. The medicine man stopped the ceremony in the middle of it. He was worried. He looked out the window toward the hill where Blah Blah was. The lightning was striking and then shooting up into the sky. He said to himself, "Oh no, you killed your brother-in-law." He was pacing the floor. Rain was falling like crazy; hail was falling. People were looking at him and thinking, "Oh no, you did it now."

Dawn broke and everything cleared up. The medicine man asked his mother-in-law, "Can we use that new tent that you have, just in case?" (He thought they might need something to wrap Blah Blah's body in). The dry creek bed was overflowing with chunks of hail and water; it was a flood. For as long as they could remember, they had never seen this happen. A bridge had to be made so they could cross. They slowly walked as if to a funeral procession, carrying the big tent. By the time they got there, it was probably about 10:00 or 11:00 in the morning. It wasn't even his time to come down. They each believed that he was dead and each one was afraid to look. Finally one of them looked and there he was with his star quilt as a pillow, the pipe was on the pipe rack on the alter. The cherry tree sticks and the tobacco ties inside were all dry but there was two feet of hail all around the perimeter.

So they brought him back in happiness knowing that this simple man named Blah Blah had done a great thing. He won the respect of the community.

SACRED FIREPLACE

From then on, they didn't make fun of him, for they knew the power of the Pipe. He held it at that time and he held it till he died.

We remember this story to reinforce our belief. The Pipe way is a journey into the light everlasting, the way and cultural belief of the Lakota.

WOUNDED KNEE - 1973

On December 29, 1890, U. S. Cavalry soldiers massacred mostly old, sick, women and children of the encampment of Chief Big Foot of the Oglala Lakota near Wounded Knee Creek. Between 300 and 500 Lakota were killed that day. On February 28, 1973, AIM (American Indian Movement) activists and local Oglala Lakota seized an old church at the Wounded Knee Massacre Site on the Pine Ridge Reservation in South Dakota for seventy-one days to protest the injustices that were happening on the reservation against the people. Their purpose was to use the seizure of the site - which for many Lakota continues to be a wound in their collective memory - as a temporary platform in hopes of ending some of the needless deaths and stealing from the people.

I want to talk about Wounded Knee 1973, touch a little bit on it because those that have been there have views of it. I know very little about it but I want to talk about it. Some people know more and they

STORIES & LESSONS

can talk about it at length, but with me it is not so much. I was not too important at that time.

I was in the hospital undergoing major surgery in January 1973 at Ellsworth Air Force Base Hospital. In that surgery, forty percent of my stomach was removed. I nearly left this world at that time. I have said why I think the Great Spirit does things so mysteriously; that when people think they can leave this world, they are kept living here. In my life, I have experienced many occasions when I could have died.

When I went through this major surgery in January 1973, I had a difficult time getting back. I was in intensive care for a long time. The time that I spent in intensive care is a story in itself because I was near death. You might say I was near the doorway of entering into the Great Hereafter but I lingered there. Drugs were inserted into me so that I would not feel the pain.

Often times, maybe because of the drugs that were given to me, I would fade away not knowing anything. But looking back on that time, I can picture it very clearly. One night I had awakened and it was pretty hard to clear the cobwebs in my brain. I was hearing a certain amount of drumming, like mumbling. When I really came conscious, I saw an old nurse, one of the ones that was taking care of me in intensive care. She was kneeling by my bedside around about the area of my knees and she was reciting the Rosary, the Catholic Prayer. I was listening to it; I got caught along with the prayer.

I thought, "How is it that a nurse, doing all she can do, taking care of a near-dying patient, can set out her heart over and beyond what she is expected to do and spend some time kneeling by the bedside of a patient and pray the Rosary?" That, to me, is doing something beyond the call of duty, beyond what she is supposed to do. It is true devotion, a true mark of her profession in trying to help a patient. She understood that the medical world in this physical world of ours was slow in making me well, and she was imploring the supernatural, the Virgin Mary, and praying the Rosary to assist me in my recovery. That to me is excellence, a shining example of the profession of a nurse tending to a patient.

When I was recovering, I had pneumonia. To make matters worse, when the bandages were removed, I wanted to scratch the wound. This was an indication that it was getting well, but then I noticed pus in between the stitches and I pointed this out to the male nurses who tended to me. They called the doctor and he cut open the stitches. This open wound infection had to be scraped off every other day and irrigated. They had to cleanse it with some medicine to help heal the infection.

I was released back to the Pine Ridge Reservation Indian Health Service Hospital and I spent several weeks there in the month of February. Because of a shortage of beds, on February 23, I volunteered to go home. I was out of intravenous feeding for over a week and able to walk around, so I thought I could manage going home. The doctor agreed with me. It would leave a bed vacant for someone else to use. But, the doctor said I was to come in every other day to have my surgery wound tended to.

STORIES & LESSONS

When I was home a couple of days, there was a meeting occurring at Calico Hall in the small community called Calico, a little over four miles north of Pine Ridge on U.S. Highway 18 going towards Hot Springs. People came to this meeting from all over the reservation. Every district had a sort of headquarters, like Oglala, Porcupine, Kyle, Manderson, *Wamble*, Allen, those places. Every district was represented there, even church people. The reason behind this meeting was Richard Wilson, chairman of the Oglala Sioux Tribal Council. He was, with the help of the BIA and the U.S. government, acting like a dictator. He had his so-called "goons" travel the highways and also the districts. These goons were keeping tabs on the people who did not like what Dick Wilson was doing.

People could not get together to communicate. We could not hold meetings. No three people could get together and talk. Even though they talked about the weather, they were broken up by Dick Wilson's goons. These goons were everywhere. Dick Wilson saw to it that everything they needed was provided for, the fuel for their cars and the whiskey that they enjoyed drinking, to give them false courage. They would go around shooting off their rifles and shooting off their mouths.

The voting precincts were heavily corrupted. Everyone on the reservation knew this. At the voting precincts, people who voted for Dick Wilson were paid in kind with a pint of wine, that sort of corruption. This was visibly observed by the people at large. When a person got drunk and got thrown in jail, he was abused, knocked around, that sort of thing. Nothing went right. There was a real power

SACRED FIREPLACE

struggle. The people knowing this got together at Calico and talked about it. In trying to put an end to this situation, they called in the American Indian Movement (AIM) to sit in on one of these meetings and try to arrive at a solution. I think it was the night of February 26. We had a secret meeting and people were chosen at random to go to the Advent Church which was just a few hundred yards from the Calico meeting hall. In the basement of the church there was quite a gathering of the people chosen to represent the districts that made up the reservation.

One of the chosen people selected to be at that meeting was myself, as sick as I was. I could not hardly sit up for twenty or twenty-five minutes at a time. I was tired, still weak, and I lost a lot of weight. All I wanted to do was lay in bed. I did not even care to eat because it was stomach surgery and a lot of the foods I was supposed to eat did not even agree with me. The recommendation of foods that I was to eat were milk and a bland sort of a soup. I could not eat fried food. Things I could eat, like potatoes, had to be steam-cooked, and that I could not eat very much. So, I was ill at ease. My disposition was not up to par.

Anyway, at that very secret meeting, the district representatives arrived at a solution. They were going to go in a car caravan and take over Wounded Knee. The thing about Wounded Knee 1890 came up in the meeting. Bits of the talk touched on Wounded Knee 1890, how the government and the 7th Cavalry committed a most shameful act in disposing of the weapons of the Indians, encircling them and then firing upon them. I believe this was the most shameful act of the

United States Government. People talk about the My Lai Massacre in Vietnam, a shameful act. My Lai happened that way, yes, but the start of My Lai in Vietnam was Wounded Knee on the Pine Ridge Indian Reservation in 1890. So, history repeats itself. The soldiers of the 7th Cavalry were honored. They were even given Congressional Medals of Honor for this cruel act of genocide.

According to our customs, our heritage, we believe we live in a world where the spirits of our relatives who have gone before us are still united very closely with us. This is how *Wakan Tanka* made us a special people. We do not ever forget our dead, most especially those that were slaughtered in the way the people were slaughtered at Wounded Knee in 1890. So, we figured that if we "in 1973" would go into Wounded Knee and take over Wounded Knee, the spirits of the dead, of our relatives of 1890, would help us. We are closely related. This is what means relationship to the Indian people.

We went back to that meeting hall in Calico and the leader told the people what we intended to do. He said we are going into Wounded Knee and anybody wishing to come along may do so. He said it in a way that was understood by the people who did not like the system we were in. With the backing of the BIA (Bureau of Indian Affairs) and the U.S. government, Dick Wilson and the Tribal Council were overruling the people. This was a wrong plainly seen by everybody. We were pushed aside, treated as if we were nothing. We were not a people to them. That was the feeling we had.

SACRED FIREPLACE

So, the people got together and they started their cars. But, like I said, I could not stay in a sitting position for more than twenty or twenty-five minutes and I was tired after the meeting at Calico Hall and the one in the basement of the church. I was overly tired and I wanted to lay down. My family and I stayed behind. When all the cars had taken off, we went along as far as our branch-off at Mission Flat and then we turned to home.

When we got home, the house was cold. We built a fire and I went straight to bed. When it was warm, I got up and stood by the stove and warmed myself. I missed the hospital, because in the hospital I did not feel the chill or unpleasantness. When I wanted medicine, they gave it to me and the room was always at average warmth. At home, we have to build a fire. Sometimes the fire is too hot, sometimes not as hot. When we go to bed at night, about an hour and a half after we all retire to sleep, the fire goes out. In the morning it is cold; it is like an ice house. Someone has to get up and start a fire.

I stood there warming myself, thinking, "Why did I ever come away from the hospital, being sickly and very weak when I could have been resting there? And in the condition I am in, why did I become involved in the cares and problems that confront the tribe? How did I become a part of the meetings and the selected group that met at the church basement?" I realized that being an Indian is the hardest thing to be in this age, as long as the dominant society has control over everything. We have to have permits for everything. And when you want to go after something, the red tape that you have to go through is so discouraging.

STORIES & LESSONS

The next day after breakfast, I wanted to go to town. I wanted to go to the court house and do some business there. When I entered the court house, a policeman told me someone wanted to see me in the BIA superintendent's office right away. We got in his car and went to the superintendent's office. When I entered his office, there was one lone Indian sitting there, it was my *tahansi* (cousin), Frank Fools Crow. We shook hands. I sat down and he said, "I do not know what they are up to but they told me to come here and here I am." So I told him, "It is the same thing with me. They told me they wanted to see me here and so I, too, came to see what was the matter."

When the superintendent came in, he told Frank and me, "The condition that we are facing now is that a car caravan has taken over Wounded Knee and roadblocks were set up so no one can come out of Wounded Knee or go into Wounded Knee. Six people have been selected to go into Wounded Knee and see the conditions there, talk to the people there, and try to negotiate a quiet settlement, so no one will get hurt and no one will get killed."

The superintendent mentioned the names of the people who were selected. There were the two Red Clouds, Charlie Red Cloud and Edgar Red Cloud. There was Frank Fools Crow and myself, Seivert Young Bear and Tom Bad Cob. These six were selected reservation-wide because we understood the part of the reservation that we lived in. And since it was a reservation-wide movement that went into Wounded Knee, we all had to talk to our people, try to negotiate with the BIA, the goon squad, and Dick Wilson's outfit.

SACRED FIREPLACE

By that time, I think the U.S. Marshals were present. I am not sure of that, but they did not waste time to get there. They wanted Frank and me to go to Wounded Knee right away. They said the other four will eventually get there. A car with a driver was provided that would take us to what they called a DMZ (demilitarized zone).

Roadblocks had been set up by the people. The roadblocks there were really efficient. There are four entrances or arteries that lead into Wounded Knee. The highway from Pine Ridge and the road from Manderson come to Wounded Knee. The road from Porcupine and the road from the Denby area and Gordon, Nebraska area come through Wounded Knee. So, there are four arteries of travel and all of these roads were blocked. The cars that went through there would have to stop and would have to be inspected. Those people not trying to help were turned back.

We came to the point called the DMZ; the AIM guards that were there stopped the car. Oscar Bear Runner was in charge of the route that goes into Wounded Knee. They came over and inspected us. They recognized us and we shook hands and explained why we came. They let us through. Frank and I had to get out of the car at that point and walk into Wounded Knee which was quite a ways, about a mile.

There were live M-16 bullets pouring into Wounded Knee at the time I went in there. Soon after arriving in Wounded Knee, we had a meeting with those that were there. We talked about the purpose of our visit. Frank asked me to talk first. I told them I was glad to see them, that I knew most

STORIES & LESSONS

of them, and being Lakota, we understand each other. That the reason I am there is that the superintendent, those in charge, perhaps the Marshals, perhaps the FBI, were eager to negotiate with those people in Wounded Knee to set their arms aside and come to terms. They wanted us to seek a negotiation where no further harm could come about. So, I talked along that line.

I said, "Deep down in my heart I am with you people. I was with you people during the meetings at Calico Hall, and the meeting held in the basement of the church close by Calico Hall. I was in this all the way through. My heart is involved, even though I am a sick man, even though I should be at home and be recuperating from this present state of my health."

Many people did not know I went through a major operation. I explained, "I am still weak and I cannot eat very much or very many foods. Even the foods I can eat by doctor's orders I cannot eat. I live in this sort of misery. But then came the call of the need to be with the Lakota people and this call was strong in my heart. I had to come because I was called upon to do something that would shake hands all around, come to an understanding, and present to the BIA, to the Marshals, to the United States government, that Dick Wilson is the cause of this taking over of Wounded Knee."

A person living like Dick Wilson is not Lakota. One of the traditions of our heritage, of the Lakota people, is that any Indian firing upon another Indian, especially with intent to kill or to do bodily harm, is not Lakota. All my life this has been my belief and all those that died in 1890 have the same

SACRED FIREPLACE

feeling. The people of the Lakota Nation, all that are traditional, will say the same words I am saying now. Those so-called Lakotas, who are the goons that fired into Wounded Knee at that time in 1973, are not Lakota. They are not Lakota. They should go away to a white community and see if they can do that over there. I would like to see that. So, I will say that what happened in Wounded Knee in 1973 will never, ever be forgiven.

    I stayed in Wounded Knee for seven days. Frank Fools Crow and the others left after the first meeting but came back almost every day. Day and night you could hear incoming M-16s and machine guns out there, rat-a-tat-tat-tat, like that. When people in the area walked in plain sight, the machine guns from the FBI roadblocks up on the hill towards Denby fired into Wounded Knee, close by where people were walking, just harassing them. The shots were fired by some ranchers living there and, of course, the Marshals and the FBI. I know they purposely did not hit anyone, but they wanted people in Wounded Knee to know they were using live bullets. They used these scare tactics to try and make the people submit to the way the dominant society wished for the outcome of Wounded Knee.

    I want to mention that the two Red Clouds, Charlie and Edgar, did not go into Wounded Knee. When the need of the people was the most, they did not heed the call to be on the side of the people who needed their help. The other three came in, Tom Bad Cobb, Seivert Young Bear, and Frank Fools Crow. They made daily trips into Wounded Knee. I remember Frank on his arrival. He had his tobacco bag. In that tobacco bag was Bull Durham and cigarettes and medicine, because he is a medicine man. He carried these inside for the people in Wounded Knee.

The FBI and the Marshals set up their own heavily guarded roadblocks. Every night, flares were sent in the direction of the Indian encampment. The local Indians knew the avenues of escape from Wounded Knee and would sneak out during the night. When they reached home, they would talk to people about conditions at Wounded Knee. They would pack up food supplies and camp goods, such as beans, rice, cornmeal, flour, baking powder, tobacco, aspirins, cold pills, and so forth. They would rest for a while, get these supplies together, put them in a knapsack, and carry them back to Wounded Knee through the night.

All the time that the siege was held by the FBI, Marshals, and Dick Wilson's goons, the traffic coming in and out of Wounded Knee at night was wide open. There are some good stories about Wounded Knee at that time. Even birds and owls helped Lakota people to find their way into Wounded Knee, or to find their way out. Many more stories of this sort I have heard during the time I was at Wounded Knee. A lot of people gathered in the church basement at Wounded Knee to be out of the cold.

It is almost always cold in the month of February on the Pine Ridge Indian Reservation. It seemed to me that the doorway was never shut for a minute, with the constant going and coming through the doorway. It was continuously open-and-shut and open-and-shut all day long and perhaps, late into the night. I was in that basement, and I noticed that everybody had the sniffles or some sort of cold. There was coughing there; we did not have medicine.

The doctor at the Indian Health Service Hospital was Dr. Nodebaum. He was a very good doctor, very close, very dedicated and devoted to the people he served. They told me that he searched for me the first day that I did not show up at Pine Ridge Hospital to have my wound cleansed and irrigated, and change bandages. He was worried about me. I was taking a terrible risk. I was old and I knew I was taking a chance.

This doctor searched for me at home and drove to places where I should be. He even went to the back alleys of Pine Ridge and to White Clay (Nebraska). He searched for me because he knew very well, being a doctor, that this open wound might get infected and maybe even cause my death. So, he searched everywhere and finally thought I might be at Wounded Knee. Under the strict supervision of the FBI, medical people were let through the roadblock to tend to the sick and carry in medicine, but that was all. They could not take foodstuffs in, only cough syrup and pills, and not to a great extent.

On the seventh day of Wounded Knee, Dr. Nodebaum went in with a medical team and had me searched out. We had called Dr. Lone Elk to come to Wounded Knee. I do not know the extent of his work at the Pine Ridge Indian Hospital, but he worked at the hospital at that time. I guess he was in the medical corps and he understands medicine and how to treat injuries. I do not know to what extent, maybe he's a real doctor, I do not know. Anyway, he knew me well because we are related. He found me sitting there in the basement of the church and he said, "Your doctor wants you outside. He has come after you and wants to take you away."

When Dr. Nodebaum found me, he shook my hands. "We missed you," he said. I rode back with him to the Pine Ridge Indian Health Service Hospital and he personally tended to my wound. He cleansed the infected area, applied medicine and bandaged it. When he was through and while I was putting my clothes on, he was sitting there on his high stool. When I was completely clothed, buttoning up my shirt and putting on my jacket, he got after me. I remember what he said.

"It is not for you to go into Wounded Knee. Look at all those others. Look outside on that road. There are young men walking that road that could be in Wounded Knee. Why are they home? For one thing, they are chicken. They do not want to go into Wounded Knee. They do not want to show themselves that they are Lakota. There are many of those people walking the streets and walking the highway, and some are at home. You are a very sick person. You should be at home because your health is the number one priority."

The doctor shook my hands again, and said, "I understand why you went in there because the people needed help, because the people were in trouble and suffering. You went in there to do your part. For this, I admire you." That is what he told me. Afterwards, Dr. Lone Elk drove me home to the Mission Flat in his car.

SACRED FIREPLACE

It was good and yet it was sad to be home, knowing what I know of Wounded Knee 1973. It was sad knowing that people there are still hungry and cold. They stayed there because they wanted to, because they did not like the setup of the tribal council that lorded over the people. Knowing what Wounded Knee was really about made me sad to be home. I wished I was able-bodied and healthy. I would have stayed at Wounded Knee from its beginning to its finish.

When I reached home, the first Saturday I went to the store to buy a few things. In the store, I met Jonas Walks—his real name is Jonas Walks Under the Ground. We know each other quite well. He came over and shook my hand. I was still a weak, sickly-looking person. He said, "I am glad to see you moving about. Try hard to get well. Tomorrow night," he said, "we are going to have a peyote meeting (Native American Church), and I personally invite you to come." So I said, "I will. Since you invite me, I will be there." Upon reaching home I told my wife, "I am invited to a peyote meeting." That Saturday night, my wife took me to where Jonas and his wife, Suzy, were living. They were the ones who held the meeting.

The meeting, they call it the Peyote Way, is a ceremony that begins in the evening, continues throughout the night until sunrise, or maybe even later than sunrise. It constitutes a lengthy service, a lengthy ceremony. I have been to these ceremonies before and I know just what to do. My wife drove me to this meeting and I told her, "Remain here, and when you see me enter the building, you can take off and go home. But, I want you to come back about eight o'clock tomorrow. I will want to go home

STORIES & LESSONS

then and lay down and rest. In this meeting we have to sit up and so I will be overly tired. So come as early as you can, so that I can get home and go to bed and rest."

I went to the outside fireplace. No one was outside but I knew that the Fire Chief, the person who tends to that fire, would come out. So, I went to the fireplace. It was a chilly night, so I was warming myself when the Fire Chief came out. He saw me and recognized me. He walked over and shook my hands. He asked me if I came for the meeting and I said, "Yes." "I will go in and talk to the leader," he said. So he went inside. After a while, he came out. "It is very crowded in there, but I have made a space beside where I am sitting and you can sit there." We started towards the building. I waved to my wife for her to go.

Around midnight, when the drum stopped, the leader Ira Elk Boy spoke. He said, "We have a new attendee here, just arrived, and we know that he was in Wounded Knee. Many of you attending this meeting have relatives in Wounded Knee, so I want him to talk a little about Wounded Knee, about the conditions there." In the silence of that crowded room, I talked about Wounded Knee. I told them how conditions were. After my talk was over, the meeting resumed.

I attended that meeting all the way through. After midnight, I was given a chance to pray out loud. In that prayer, I implored the Great Spirit, *Wakan Tanka*, to bless the people at Wounded Knee, to give them courage and strength, and help them. Some had families at home. Some had children at home attending school who were left in the care of

SACRED FIREPLACE

relatives. I was very grateful that they gave me a special invitation to attend this meeting so that I could pray for those who were in Wounded Knee.

The eyes and ears of the whole world were focused on Wounded Knee, and this is one fact why the Marshals, the FBI, and Wilson's goons did not rush into Wounded Knee to annihilate the Lakotas who were there like they did in 1890. They did not kill the spirit of Wounded Knee 1890, and they did not kill the spirit of Wounded Knee 1973. There is unrest and there is misunderstanding causing the misery for Native Americans, but the Lakota shall go on as long as *Wanka Tanka*, the Great Spirit, watches over us.

Many tribes, even our neighbors, the Mexicans, found their way into Wounded Knee. And from all directions—north, south, east, and west—local people took time out to take people who have never been in Wounded Knee and guide them in. When people wished to leave, the local people who knew the terrain led them out. They knew the ways to get around the roadblocks, and the ways to hide when the flares were lit. At one point during my stay in Wounded Knee, a heavy bomber came from the south. All the men that had firearms, which were mainly .22s, they fired at this bomber. No matter how small the weaponry the Lakota had, or how unequal in numbers, facing the forces of a mighty opposition, the fight in the heart of the Lakota was strong.

I am glad that I spent just seven days and seven nights in Wounded Knee 1973. I am glad I did my bit. When the two Red Clouds were asked to help out in our misery and did not show up, they failed

STORIES & LESSONS

the people. Six of us were selected to do this work and they were the only two who did not show up. Four of us went, and two Red Clouds did not go. How can we look to them to be leaders of this Sioux Nation? They have shown at Wounded Knee 1973, that they did not answer that call, the call to help the people get over this rough stuff, get over this trying time. I do not look to the Red Clouds as leaders. They might be smart in talking; they might even holler and be loud, but they did not show up in Wounded Knee 1973. That proves that they are not leaders of the Lakota Nation.

Several times during this occupation, it is known by many people that Dick Wilson said, "I have my ninety guns that will march into Wounded Knee and wipe it out." What do you think about that? It would be a repetition of Wounded Knee 1890 - this time Dick Wilson's goons and not the 7th Cavalry, it would be Dick Wilson's goons that would have done that. I think the conscience of the Marshals and the FBI were, at least to a point, clear that if Dick Wilson was allowed to do this, it would be known all over the world because of the press and television people. The BBC, ABC, NBC, CBS, all of these people, were inside Wounded Knee. They knew we had a lot of people talking of the conditions that were evident in Wounded Knee 1973.

Several books have been written about Wounded Knee, but I think that those people who were in Wounded Knee know for themselves that what is written in these books is not all there. I have stated what I thought about it in an Indian Way. We have among us a percentage of the goons and their children that are still with us. The problem is still

SACRED FIREPLACE

here. It will be here until the day the Great Spirit sees to it in His merciful love to change the way of life at the so-called end of the world.

I can still recall how it was at Wounded Knee in 1973. People from all over - Canada, the state of Washington, California, the Southwest. There is a great love there, we understood each other. We were hungry together, we were tired together, we were cold together. We know what brotherhood is because we lived it. We know the meaning of love. Buddy LaMont gave his life during the course of his stay in Wounded Knee 1973. Frank Clearwater, another Indian from some tribe out east, gave his life. There are others, a girl from Nova Scotia died.

Through the years after Wounded Knee 1973, some young men and some young women gave their lives for what happened in Wounded Knee. They were very special people. Pedro Bisonette was one of them. He was a leader of the Oglala Sioux civil rights organization. Anna Mae Aquash paid with her life, too. The Pine Ridge goons or the police murdered them; we know this. But the record on this says differently, very differently.

These wrongs will have to be answered and paid for. They are not forgiven. I do not think those people in Wounded Knee who were there and suffered along in Wounded Knee 1973 have ever forgiven what the FBI, the Marshals, and Dick Wilson's goons have done to us. Before I have said that forgiveness is one of the greatest acts of mercy, of compassion, of love that any person can do. But our tradition and our beliefs that we live by, this heritage of ours since *Wakan Tanka* placed us here in this world, says that any Lakota who fires

STORIES & LESSONS

upon another Lakota is not Lakota, and shall never again be Lakota. For myself there is no forgiveness. So, we know where we stand.

Are we Lakota or not? We are Lakota and nothing can change that. If we are not, well we are just not Lakota. It is as simple as that. It is a way of life that *Wakan Tanka*, the Great Mystery, gave to us, and we understand that. We lived it, we suffered in it. This thought sings in the hearts of people that were in Wounded Knee in 1973. This cradle of life that the Great Spirit protects us in will continue for as long as this Earth is our Mother. And when the Great Spirit, in His merciful love, makes changes in this world that we always refer to as the end of the world, there will be an answering of the wrongs. The Lakota that fired upon another Lakota will have to answer. I do not care what kind of a religion they turn to in order to hide their bad conscience, they will answer for the bullets that they slung into the Indian encampment at Wounded Knee 1973.

The fires of Wounded Knee are still burning. They shall burn to that time when this Earth is changed altogether. They will burn shiny in front of the face of the Great Spirit. And those who have given their lives, we shall never forget them. We may forget their names, but their spirit is still here with us. They have come close to us; they have become our relations, now and forever. This is the Lakota way - this is the tradition that we are accustomed to.

SACRED FIREPLACE

Petaga Yuha Mani, 1990

TRIP TO ATLANTA - 1990

Pete Catches was active in the civil rights movement at the same period as Dr. Martin Luther King, Jr. In Pete's view, King was a "dog soldier," or a warrior who placed himself in harm's way to protect his people. In 1990 in Atlanta, Georgia, the King family adopted Pete, and in 1991, he was presented with the Martin Luther King Freedom Award in Washington, D.C.

STORIES & LESSONS

Dr. Martin Luther King, Jr., is a man whom I look up to with deep respect as a man of the people. I would call Dr. King a true warrior and leader who put his life on the line to help the suffering and forgotten people of this world. I have stated before that Dr. Martin Luther King, Jr., threw his lance into the ground on the battlefield and tethered himself to the lance, and vowed never to leave until the battle was won. And, as is the common fate of the greatest warriors and leaders of this world, he sacrificed his life for his people and his belief that the Creator put us all here as equal human beings, none above the rest.

In the winter of 1990, I was privileged to be among several Native American spiritual leaders and representatives invited to meet with board members and staff of the Martin Luther King, Jr., Center for Nonviolent Social Change, to discuss how the African American and Native American communities could work together to resolve problems of mutual concern, including domestic issues and the global issue of achieving world peace. The meeting took place during King Week 1990, the celebration of the sixty-first birthday and the fifth national holiday honoring Reverend Dr. Martin Luther King, Jr., in Atlanta, Georgia. I was put in the position of being elder statesman and spiritual leader for the Native American assemblage. I never did feel comfortable being put in this kind of position. I feel better being at the back, just being part of the group. I was asked to tape a message for the Indian students at Chemawa Indian School in Oregon. I also spoke at the Ecumenical services on Dr. King's birthday.

SACRED FIREPLACE

I have been invited back to the King Center and been invited to be a part of the King family. This experience is something in my life that I never thought might happen, even in my dreams. I will be steadfast in my support of everyone associated with the King Center. I want to do my best to live up to my commitment. My prayers will always be with Coretta Scott King and all the King family

MESSAGE TO CHEMAWA INDIAN STUDENTS

A message to all Native American students . . .

I feel honored. I feel good. I have a good feeling that this day is special, a memorial to Dr. Martin Luther King, Jr., and his philosophy and ideas in life. It should go all over the world, especially to young people. Those of you that are sitting in class now have a future to look to, and this being a special day, I want to impart unto you a blessing of the Great Spirit, to let you understand and see what is good and beautiful in life. That in your life you would adhere to the principles that are good, the things that will manifest itself into something to help other people to get on the Red Road of Life.

As young students, you have the great opportunity to grow up into a strong generation, a generation that will be smarter than the previous generation. The same is true of the oncoming generations behind you. This is called tradition, a heritage that was given to us by the Great Spirit. We must keep it alive, we must work hard, and we must help each other.

I do not see you now, but in my mind, I can picture every one of you. This is the work of the

STORIES & LESSONS

Great Spirit. I am talking directly to you, hoping that you will grasp something from this message and carry on that banner, or that torch, or that idea. We are in a march for peace. And in order to get that peace, we must love one another. We must work together, see each other, not in color, not in culture, but as true brothers of one family under God. It will be a hard road for some of us. But, the effort must be there. It will be hard sometimes to stay on the right path, but remember always that the Great Spirit is beside you.

The answer to problems throughout our lives are within each of us. in whatever age or time we may come upon problems, but the answers to those problems are within us. They are lying there dormant. We have to stir them up. We have to seek the answer to the problems that assail us. And in that way, knowing this, knowing that the Great Spirit is with us, we can surely and truly be a part of a movement for world peace.

We all have a job to do. We should not leave anything unturned to do that job and put our efforts together. I see in all of you the resemblance of Christ because He is in us, and we are in Him. The goodness that is in you, let it shine. Continue that way, ever bright, full of love, so beautiful, as part of His Creation. Look around you and enjoy His creation - His light, this daylight, the stars at night, the moon, the sun, the air. All this is beautiful. Use it well.

Do not revert to alcohol and drugs. Stay away from them. Whenever you have an urge to resort to alcohol and drugs, think of this old man who has experienced drunkenness. This man who was a

SACRED FIREPLACE

drunk himself at one time, but has come away and committed his whole life, the remaining portion of his life, in sobriety. You, too, can do that.

You are beautiful. Whatever is in you is beautiful. Live with it. Enjoy the things that are around you, the food that you eat, the water that you drink, the air that you breathe. As you gaze in the far distant horizon, see the lightning and hear the thunder, the voice of the Great Spirit. He is that close to you. When you walk, you walk on the Mother Earth, you walk on the bosom of our Mother, the Earth.

So today I am privileged to say these very few words, words of love, for you. May the Great Spirit bless you. May His love shine upon you and guide you through life, direct you, make you strong, make you love one another. Because love is a tool for peace. We have to have love first, love of our neighbor, to know what peace is. We cannot have peace with Star Wars. We cannot have peace with conquering of minorities. We can have peace no other way than to love one another. Even the Christmas message the angels brought—peace on earth, good will to men—is not only meant at Christmas time. It is meant for all of our lives, every day of our life. And we must strive to keep in mind the principles that are so valuable, the virtues that are ever present that we can use - honesty and truthfulness, love for one another, obedience, long suffering, perseverance. These are values that we have to live by and share with each other. This is love.

Love comes in many ways. Love is not just when you kiss one another. No. You love the flowers, you love the running streams, you love the mountains,

STORIES & LESSONS

you love the sunshine, and the chill of the winter wind. This is love. We are part of this nature. So, let us be one with nature. The way the Great Spirit created nature was beautiful in all its goodness. The streams were running pure and clean; the mountaintops with their snow caps were pure. With all the factories, the rivers are now polluted - the fish drift downstream, their lives gone because of pollution. We can change this. The Great Spirit created this universe.

We have come to an age where we have to stand together and understand each other in order to help each other. We ask ourselves, "How can I be of help to others?" You can be a role model in whatever age you are, whether you are a teenager, or in the twenties or thirties. You do not have to advertise, "I do not drink alcohol, I do not use drugs." You do not have to say that. You can live it and people will notice. They will see that you are living a good life. They will see that you go out of your way to do things that are right. They will understand you. They will love you for that. And I think that when you live that way, it is the Red Road of Life.

When you get up in the morning, the first thought that enters your mind should be one of thankfulness that you awoke on another beautiful day. Be thankful that you are privileged to enjoy another day. When food is on the table, be thankful that you are able to eat some of it. When you take a drink of water, bless yourself with this water, because water, too, is sacred. There is no one, not a living thing, that can stay alive without water. It is so important, this water, that when we partake of it and drink some, we respect it. Our love touches it. This is love.

In our daily lives, we should continue with utmost care to be this role model. I know that sometimes it is going to be hard to do this. I should know at my age. Some days seem dreary and bleak. But look around you. The old medicine man that taught me said this: "Look to nature, because nature will teach you. The power of the earth, the power of the sea, two separate things, each having its own separate power. We are part of that, the cycle that we live. The water that flows down the river will return some day. It will flow to the ocean, and it will go up into the atmosphere and in the form of rain and snow, come back to us again."

So, too, life is a cycle. We begin at birth, we continue to live a complete life, and when we get to old age, we arrive back where we started. We become feebleminded, losing our sight and our hearing and our teeth. If we become too aged, we crawl on all fours like the babies we were at one time. This is life. It revolves in a cycle. From where it began, we arrive back to that place. We come from the Great Spirit through Mother Earth, and to Her we shall return some day.

Before we return to Mother Earth, we have this life to live. Why not live this life in the goodness of the Great Spirit the way He meant for us to live, in a beautiful environment, in a beautiful way. We can do it. I know you can do it. It is in you to do what needs to be done. And I am sure, guided by the Great Spirit, His blessing and His grace, you can live a good life and be that role model in whatever age bracket you live. In this fashion, others will follow you. You need to plant that seed. You need to grow into that model. So from that, others will follow.

I will close here with a prayer that will include all of you, in my own tongue, in my own way, as the Great Spirit intended me to pray. I have those thoughts and what I have told you on my mind, imploring the Great Spirit to bless each and every one of you, your families, your homes, your lives in the future. And may His love be always upon you.

So I leave you with a great love in my heart for you. May the Great Spirit love you, bless you in everything that you do, in every way that you wish to live your future life.

Ecumenical Services

Dr. Martin Luther King, Jr., Birthday and Holiday Celebration, Atlanta, Georgia, 1990

I love you, every one of you. I came here because I wanted to. Yesterday was the day that I was to do a ceremony on the Rosebud Reservation. I was given notice of that ceremony quite a while before hand, but I chose to come here. It is important that I would be among you on this 61st birthday and holiday of Dr. Martin Luther King, Jr., that the flower of freedom will include the red race, this beautiful flower of His creation.

The flower of freedom began with one root and now it is becoming united to form one cause - the March of Freedom. Just as the walls of Eastern Europe and elsewhere have shaken and fallen down, so too may the walls of misunderstanding

SACRED FIREPLACE

and of poverty be shaken and crumble and fall, to unite us all in one family, in one beautiful flower as the Lord intended it to be.

That flower is the flower of love. That flower is the flower of understanding. It is so pure it will ascend its perfume throughout the whole world in the blessing of the Great Spirit, the Lord of all people and nations. I will pray now.

Four (Topa)

CEREMONIES

RADIANTLY I COME

by Zintkala Oyate

From antiquity, the genesis of our belief begins with three warriors scouting for buffalo. This is the main sustenance of the Lakota. It was a very hot season and the buffalo herds stayed in the cooler north and the *Ka Sapa*, which is known as the Black Hills.

The people were bewildered for this was *Wipazuntka Waste Wi* (June). The prairie grass reached high and touched a maiden's long beautiful hair at the waist. Yet, where were the buffalo?

In the *Oyate*, the people knew they had a *nagi* or spirit or ghost that was their true selves. This is what the dreamers told them. This was a time before the horses came. In that time, the dreamers knew the constellations; the evening star, the morning star, and they lived the proper fashion of balance. They lived the proper fashion of balance with goodness.

Now these three warriors came to a little stream upon which to drink some fresh cool water and eat some *wacakampi* (smoked dried meat) from their pouches. It is then they heard this rumbling. It was

SACRED FIREPLACE

towards the West, standing they looked that way. They saw this hill and upon this hill they saw something strange was happening. They were drawn towards this hill in the West. The warriors started walking in that direction except for one who was the youngest and fastest. In case something unfortunate happened to the older two, he would run and tell the encampment what he saw and knew.

They saw a Mist gathering in the blueness of the sky. At first, it glowed greenish as it came spiraling down, then a reddish hue, then it wavered there.

The two scout warriors approached the hill with its beautiful pine trees. They noticed the soundless surroundings, only a calm quiet breeze. They watched in fearful anguish, and trembling, they stopped.

Once again continuing down, changing again to a bright golden yellow, resting finally, the mist had become a pure white, silverish grey aura.

In one's heart, this is an equinox of our lives. An emotion so prevalent to our spirit happened, and its Essence that was inside of us. We are the good people. We get truthfulness; we get honesty. We see this Mist in our heart and our loneliness is gone.

There is a fortitude in how our whole family is. This whole world is because of *Wakan Tanka* (Great Mystery) and because of *Pte San Win*. The happiness that we feel with the family is not in engagement.

We see Her and our spirit becomes One with the Creator because *Pte San Win* is His Daughter. Our

CEREMONIES

life's blood is matriarchal and that is the time that we understand.

A whirlwind descended that was Holy. It had come to Her People, the People of Peace. The Beauty of Life had now appeared.

"Why was this Woman here alone?" One of the two had bad thoughts and the mysterious cloud enveloped the two. One of the two, his bones lay there bleached, the one with the bad thoughts. Then the other one laid down on the ground, for in his heart, he knew She was from *Wakan Tanka*. She said to him, "Rise and go back to your people and get a place ready for Me. Tell them I am *Pte San Win* and that my Father has sent Me. I will appear in four days time, now go."

It is an empathy of how our souls grow into modernity; how the People of Peace formed into a great nation. The bravery embedded in us will always be there because it is given to us as a whole spiritual essence.

We have become One with the nature of ourselves. It is integral to understand the meaning, awesome magnanimity, the Rites She had brought to the People of Peace.

From the North She comes, roles towards the West, and back to the North. Where the Sun rises in the East, and South where the warm winds come from, She becomes the Holiness of Her Father... *PTE SAN WIN*. The order of communal aspiration can only be achieved in the service of GOD'S OWN LIGHT.

In the depth of our jungle of fears comes an Enlightenment to conjure our despair away, in order

SACRED FIREPLACE

to live in the guidance of the Seven Sacred Rites underneath the magnificent Sun. She has come to give a true Reality of an enduring Love to Her People of Peace.

In the moment of the Radiant Glow that She has brought, comes an awakening in the Teepee of our Grandfathers who have called in songs and pertinent prayers to bless our ways. Now seven Rites are in us to live beautifully.

In the health of her people, She brought a Sacredness in a bundle with the forearm of a buffalo calf, the *Sacred* Pipe. For generations to come, the will completes this Holy Design. Now a song entwines a balanced harmony, heard by many and joyously understood to those who will receive its Splendor. A few certain multitude can clasp its Dignity, this Radiance emitting from Her.

    Radiantly I come
    Radiantly I come
    Radiantly I come
      Your Grandfathers have asked Me to come.
    Radiantly I come
    Radiantly I come
    Radiantly I come
      Your Grandfathers' altar will I appear.
    Radiantly I come
      Radiantly I send goodness
      Radiantly I bring Health and Happiness.

CEREMONIES

Petaga Yuha Mani filling his *Sacred* Pipe

THE SEVEN SACRED RITES

The Lakota have many rites and ceremonies, but there are seven major sacred rites given to the Lakota by *Pte San Win* (Buffalo Calf Woman). The seven are: the Purification Rite (Inipi), Pipefast (Hanbleceya), Sundance (Wiwangyang Wacipi), Making of the Buffalo Woman (also known as the Coming of Age), Throwing of the Sacred Ball, Making of a Relative, and Keeping and Releasing the Spirit. Four of the seven will be discussed, and the remaining three are briefly described below.

The Coming of Age, or Making of the Buffalo Woman, is a rite solely for young women who have reached puberty. Medicine women carry out this long four day ceremony. Because Lakota society is matriarchal, there is a sacred ceremony dedicated

SACRED FIREPLACE

exclusively to women. (There is no comparable ceremony for men.)

The Throwing of the Sacred Ball ceremony is carried out when the Lakota Nation's survival is at stake. This ceremony is not being held or directed by a medicine man at the present time, but may be reintroduced if the need arises in the future

Finally, the Keeping and Releasing of the Spirit ceremony is aimed at restoring communal unity, that is, to heal the shattered unity of families. For this ceremony, the medicine man spends time with members of the family and advises them on what they should do to heal the unity of the family over a one-year period. After the year has ended, certain rituals are conducted.

CEREMONIES

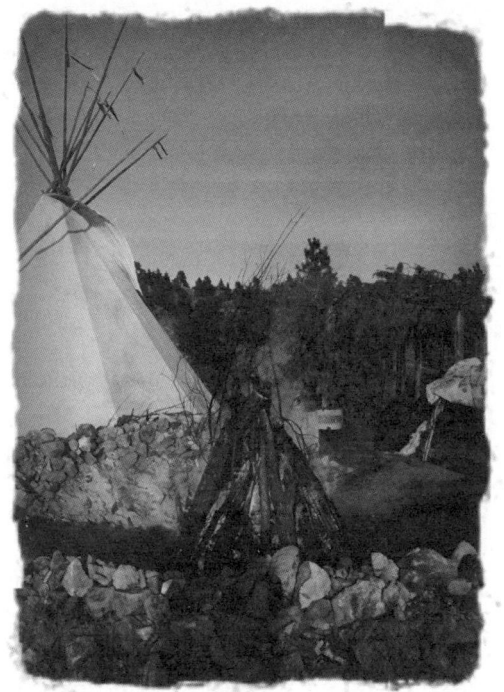

Preparing for Inipi Ceremony

Inipi (Purification Rite)
The First Form of Prayer

I think that the name "sweat lodge" is not the proper name for this sacred rite. We should not devalue the rite with a common word like "sweat." It is a sacred rite and it should be kept in that sphere. Of course, we do sweat in a sweat lodge, but the proper name for the rite is *Inipi* (Purification).

SACRED FIREPLACE

As oral history points out to us, the Purification Rite is the oldest form of prayer of the Native aboriginals of North America. Included are people in Mexico, the fifty states, and Canada, even Alaska. In my travels to the many states, I have come upon Alaskan Eskimos that enjoy going into a sweat lodge with us. Being Natives, the original inhabitants of this Western Hemisphere, the sweat lodge is the first form of prayer that natives know in seeking the Great Spirit's blessing and help.

The sweat lodge, so to speak, is very important to us. I see the Purification Rite as very important in the life of the Lakota people, especially for those that have anything to do with the Pipe. Purification of body, mind, emotions, and spirit is important for those who want Pipe ceremonies, go to the Sundances, have naming ceremonies for their children, doctor members of their family, or in the sad event of losing someone who has gone from this world into the next, because we like to bury them in this way. It is so important we purify ourselves for any given ceremony by going into the sweat lodge. This is so the Great Spirit will come to the occasion and bless our ceremony, bless our Pipe, our prayers, our lives, whatever the occasion may be, whether it be a happy occasion, or whether it be a sad occasion. So, the sweat lodge is very important.

Whenever weather permits, we should go into the Purification Rite, because, when we purify ourselves—bodies, minds, and spirits—we can come close to the Great Mystery. We know He loves us. He created us. He fashioned this world for us. He wants us to live this way. He gave us these rites. Through these rites we can talk to Him, implore and ask Him favors, receive a healing, and

CEREMONIES

receive help for the things that we are troubled with. To me, the sweat lodge is so powerful, so good, so lovely, so in peace. You will find peace; you will experience peace in the sweat lodge.

My trailer camp, where I live, is a poor place, situated nine miles north of Pine Ridge on Highway 18, going towards Hot Springs, and off to your left about a half mile. On a little table (butte) of land stands a small trailer, one of these old-time traveling trailers that they pull behind a pickup truck or a car. This summer we had what is known as a squaw cooler—a shade made out of pine boughs, so we could sit there and enjoy visiting through the hot day. That little table seems to get a heck of a lot of wind, and through the summer months, we experienced some heavy wind and our squaw cooler toppled over. My sweat lodge is situated just a few yards south of the squaw cooler, and it is fenced in with woven wire. This is how much I respect the area that is immediately around my sweat lodge. I do not allow dogs or cats near that area. Every person knows that dogs will go and pee on anything. So, in my mind long years ago, I fashioned in my mind, that when I have a sweat lodge I will fence it up with woven wire to keep dogs and cats away so that the *Tunkasilas*, the *tunkas*, the rocks that are to be used, will not be desecrated. The wood that will be used to burn at the fire pit will be protected, as well as the canvases over the frame of the sweat lodge. But most of all, I want to protect that little mound of dirt in front of the opening of the sweat lodge which is most especially sacred to me. Even when I just go and clean my fire pit of ashes, I stop at the gate

SACRED FIREPLACE

and look over the area and check to see that all is well.

As I mentioned before, we have strong winds through there, and my sweat lodge covering is scattered here and there, torn from its frame. It can probably stand one more year. The canvas and the rugs lie on the ground. The snow and the rain have frozen them to the ground and they could not be straightened out, so I left them that way. But the frame is intact. The reverence, the thought of a sacred place still lingers there. My wife takes her tobacco ties there, places it in the sweat lodge, and prays. Even though over these many months the rocks in the center from the last sweat lodge have gone cold since the first snow, we still touch the rocks with reverence. When we offer our tobacco ties and our Bull Durham, we touch the stones.

Towards the setting sun further west from the entrance of the sweat lodge and the mound is the fire pit. The fire pit signifies an old man. It is shaped like a horseshoe, or a face. When you clean your fire pit of ashes, sprinkle them along the outer edges. After you have sweat lodge ceremonies a dozen or more times, you will see the resemblance of an old man, graying hair, dark in places, but graying mostly. Mother Earth and that old man, which is the fire of life, go together, hand-in-hand, on this Red Road of Life. Around the fire pit, you sprinkle ashes of the last used fire pit, a constant reminder that we shall return to dust at the end of our lives.

CEREMONIES

Pete's brother, Joe, carrying in the *Tunkas*

PREPARATIONS FOR *INIPI*

Long ago when the old-timers went out to gather sage in preparation for a sweat lodge, they would bring back huge armfuls of sage. They did not make just one trip. They would go out on foot, way out somewhere, way out on the plains where the sage is fresh and pure. They would bring it back and put a matting on the ground inside the sweat lodge. The more time you put in preparing a sweat lodge, the better. Every breath that you take while you are working there is a prayer. The thoughts that

SACRED FIREPLACE

you have while you are working are a part of the prayer. Every step, every motion that you undertake, is part of the prayer of the sweat lodge to be held.

The old-timers would go out and bring back two rocks, walking back every step. In the old days, the Indians took *wasa* (red paint made from clay) with them. They prayed and then painted the rocks that they were going to take home. They talked to the rocks because at one time, ages and ages ago, *Wakan Tanka* made them. The rocks might have been very big at one time, even as big as a house, but over time became small. But through these rocks, the prayer will be bigger than a house, maybe big enough to bring health to some person. They carried two at a time, and placed them near the fire pit. They made several trips. One person did that. Then they would gather wood. They would go out in the hills, cut wood over there, and haul it back by hand, carrying it on their shoulders. This is how it was done.

In this day and age we drive out in a pickup, gather the sage, the rocks, the wood, all in one shot. They might even bring back thirty, forty, fifty rocks, half a pickup truck load of wood, and a whole bunch of sage. And while doing this, they will have a cigarette in their mouths. That is not reverence for something for the Purification Rite that is being prepared. I see this often, and I have spoken against it.

The *Sacred* Pipe must be filled before a sweat lodge ceremony. The Pipe will be brought in and smoked during the ceremony. The true way to fill a Pipe is to begin by singing the Pipe-filling song.

CEREMONIES

When the medicine man offers this pinch of *cansasa* to the West and prays, he prays for all of the ones that are going in and their families, whatever their needs may be. He offers *cansasa* to the Four Directions, to *Wanble Gleska* (Spotted Eagle), and to our Mother Earth. When he is through filling the Pipe, he stands up with it and offers it to the Four Directions, to the Heavens above, and to our Mother the Earth.

In order for it to be a good ceremony, when you fill the Pipe, you should pray in the Lakota tongue, the native tongue that *Wakan Tanka* gave to us. He did not give you the English language. That is foreign, that is another race, it belongs somewhere else. The Lakota way is the Red Road of Life. Only if we do it correctly will He bless our ceremonies, will He answer our prayers.

INSIDE THE *INIPI*

I see many mistakes by "modern" Indians in conducting a sweat lodge ceremony. When you go into a sweat lodge ceremony, you must close your lips. Nowadays, even at Sundance sweat lodges, some people joke inside of a sweat lodge. This old man, who I will speak about later, told me this: "The rocks have no eyes; they have no ears; they have no mouth. But they see you, they hear you. They echo your prayer to the Great Spirit. So, when the spirits are there, you should sit there with reverence, reverence for yourself, respect for yourself, and respect to be one of the honored participants of a sweat lodge ceremony. A person

SACRED FIREPLACE

should be silent. They should sit there in silent devotion when the rocks are brought in."

When a medicine man begins praying, and when he sings a song, we should support him, sing along. Even though we do not know the song, we should hum, following his tune. In order to be perfect, in order to have power, we must become as one. We must all work together. If it is only half of the people in the sweat lodge are enthused in a ceremony, and the other half have their minds on something else, such as women, money, jobs, things other than what is taking place, the rite is only half as powerful as it could be. When everyone, all of the people that are in a sweat lodge, go along and work together and pray together, then they are one—solid and strong—to implore the Great Spirit for His love so that He will take care of us.

When the Pipe is brought in after two door openings, I often see individuals sitting there going through the motions of pointing to the Four Directions, to the Mother Earth, and touching the rocks and killing a lot of time. The medicine man has already done that. So, when the Pipe is to be smoked inside, why should everyone sit there and be motioning to the Four Directions and to the rocks and to whatever? That is not necessary; it has already been done.

I could go on and on talking about the sweat lodge, the Purification Rite, but I see so many mistakes in many places that I have visited. In some places where I was invited to a sweat lodge ceremony, some of them come out after each door opening because they cannot stand the heat, and

CEREMONIES

they go back in before it is shut tight again. I feel that this is wrong. I think that when you enter a sweat lodge before the ceremony starts, you should remain in there until the final conclusion and then come out. The Purification Rite to me is a sacred ceremony, a solid way of prayer in part, because it involves suffering.

I know that what I am saying here seems not right to some other tribes. I respect their way of conducting a sweat lodge. I have heard that in certain places, the sweat lodge door opening seven times. I think this is beautiful practice, because we have Seven Sacred Rites (Purification Rite, Pipefast, Sundance, Making of the Buffalo Woman, Throwing of the Ball, Making of a Relative, and, Releasing of the Spirit). In the Spotted Eagle's Way, the way that I am talking about, the way I learned, the sweat lodge entrance doorway faces the west. Let me say that there are other doorways. There is a doorway toward the north; there is a doorway towards the east; there is a doorway towards the south; and there is even a doorway in the ceiling of a sweat lodge. These have to do with the many other sacred rites of other medicine men (bear, elk, *heyhoka, yuwipi, and so on).* They have different doorways. But in the Spotted Eagle Pipe Way, the sweat lodge doorway faces the west.

Because, if we do things differently, we are weak. That is the answer to many of our problems. If all of us would unite and do it one way, have one mind, one language, one song, while praying together, we will be loved by the Great Spirit and become strong. This is the Pipe Way; whoever uses the Pipe in the proper way, honoring it, cherishing it, loving it, living with it, taking care of it,

SACRED FIREPLACE

and thinking that it is a priceless gift, He will give to us whatever our needs may be. No matter how many horses, cars, or homes we may have, the Pipe is far more precious.

GOOD LANCE'S TEACHINGS

The old one (Good Lance) who taught me this medicine way of life told me this: "These rocks that you call *tunkan* have no eyes, have no ears, and have no mouths, but it is through these that we pray to the Great Spirit. When we enter a sweat lodge, these same rocks implore the Great Spirit to see us, they hear our prayer, they implore the Great Spirit to receive our prayer. They are the intercessors. Through the heat of the sweat lodge, the rocks transcend the prayer of the Lakota to the Great Spirit."

Good Lance told me also that the dirt mound in front of the entrance of the sweat lodge is a huge mountain. We see a small dirt pile, maybe twelve inches high. But when the spirits come, the supernatural, this little pile of dirt is like a mountain. The top of this little dirt pile reaches into the heavens, into the world beyond, into the domain of the Great Spirit.

The old man beckoned me to go with him as he was going to tell me something. He said, "Little brother, this little mound of dirt that you can step over in this physical world, there are many good men and good women that could not come up to the top, to the summit, of this small mound of dirt.

CEREMONIES

In the supernatural spirit way, this mound reaches into the heavens and beyond, into the domain of the Great Spirit. Little brother, whatever you do, try and strive to get to that summit. You have all your life to climb it, and someday you will stand on the pinnacle of this summit, of this huge mountain that rises above this vast world.

"There are many good men and many good women that just go part way, and stumble and fall all the way down. There is a route, a path, known as the Pipe Trail. There is a path, the same path, that is known as the medicine way of life—curing the sick, helping those who have problems and who are in need. If you follow that path, someday you will reach the top. In the effort to get to the top, some are overly anxious and they tumble down, clear to the base and beyond. Their second effort is much harder than the first. Even, little brother, if you have to crawl on your belly, using your elbows to crawl up that huge mountain, do it. Even if you skin your elbows, even if there are tears in your eyes, even if your tribulations are so heavy that it tries to pull you down to this earth that we are so accustomed to, try, try.... And in the effort of trying, you may even shed tears. Up on the summit someday, the Great Spirit will accept your Pipe, if you use it right.

"The pathway of this Pipe Way and medicine way is your Lakota way of life—your language, your way, your culture, your tradition, your heritage. You have to speak Lakota. This is the way, the Red Road of Life. The beginning is the sweat lodge ceremony, and all through your life you will have to follow that pathway, the Red Road of Life."

SACRED FIREPLACE

The talk of the Pipe Way, *Cannunpa Tawooglake*, says this: "Whoever respects this Pipe, honors it, takes care of it, loves it, will have along life. He will one day walk with three legs (meaning walk with a cane), and if he continues to live that beautiful way of life, someday, even though his eyesight is gone, his teeth are gone, his ears are no more, he may walk like an animal with four legs, using two canes.

"The Pipe Way is a beautiful way, and it is a hard way. There are many difficult times along the way, that long journey up that hill where good men and good women topple and roll down to the base."

Good Lance told me someday I would understand. It was perhaps five or six years after he left this world that I understood what he told me that day about that little hill in front of the doorway of the sweat lodge.

In order to love all of the sweat lodge - the frame, the coverings, the little pile of dirt in front of the doorway, and the fire pit, Good Lance also told me, "Do not leave the fire pit, because the fire, the air, the water, and the earth are four of the most essential things of life, and this is part of the Lakota prayer. Around the fireplace is health. Around the fireplace is a new rebirth, children coming into the world. Around the fire pit is a place that you should go, whether there is a fire in it in preparation for a sweat lodge, or whether you get up early in the morning and walk to the sweat lodge area. Go to the fire pit and look around, see the old man looking at you, a constant reminder that we have one life, that some day our hair will be as white as what we are seeing." So, I do this. It is a beautiful way of life, a way that is the beginning of any Lakota ceremony.

A WAY OF LIFE

Earlier I mentioned that the Lakota religion is very unique, a thing apart, not like the other religions where they have a membership drive and things like that. We can go to a sweat lodge ceremony and partake of the ceremony, and then, we can stay away for a whole year, or two or three. According to circumstances, a person might be at work, he might be under contract somewhere, or he might be in a foreign country where sweat lodges are not known. He might be away for five or six years, but when he comes back, he can go to a sweat lodge. He is as welcome to go there as the first time that he went.

When walking the pathway, the Red Road of Life, we should each day do it right to our utmost ability, to be certain that what we do is right and aboveboard, nothing hidden, nothing sneaky, nothing underhanded. The Great Spirit fashioned the path and gave it to us. He sees everything we do, what we think in the sweat lodge, how we pray. He decides whether it shall grow? Shall He bless the prayers that we say? Shall He bless us, bless our ceremony?

Lakota religion is so unique; it is like a tree, one type of tree, the Tree of Life, that *Wakan Tanka* planted. Its roots are there in a sweat lodge. Its foundation is the rocks in the center, tempered with

SACRED FIREPLACE

heat, tempered with prayer, tempered with sacred songs. And as it grows, it glows red like the color of the fire. And how we live, using the sweat lodge in our life, is the way that tree will ascend before *Wakan Tanka*, for Him to see what our life was really like.

What I have tried to explain here is about the Red Road of Life, about respect for the sweat lodge, the deep devotion that we should have when we go in a sweat lodge. When we enter a sweat lodge we have to focus with our minds. The prayers that we will say must be in Lakota. When the Buffalo Calf Woman brought the *Sacred* Pipe to the Lakota people many centuries ago, She did not bring it to an English-speaking people. The Creator, *Wakan Tanka*, brought the Pipe to a Lakota-speaking people and that is how it is meant to be.

I am not saying that non-Indians should not go to a sweat lodge. No. I am not saying that. It is my belief that those white people that go to the sweat lodge ceremonies were, in their former lives, Natives themselves, because we strongly believe in reincarnation. The only thing is that, if they want to continue in this Indian ceremonial way, attend sweat lodges, go on a Pipefast and be a part of a Sundance, they should learn Lakota. I repeat, I do not care if they are white people. If they want to Sundance, if they want to Pipefast, if they want to take part in the sweat lodge ceremony, they should learn Lakota, and I do not mean maybe. Absolutely! It is easy to learn the language. When you learn the Lakota language, you know that you have entered into the realm of a unique religion, a religion that is of its own, very beautiful, of this Western Hemisphere. It did not come from overseas. It was from this Western Hemisphere that the Lakota religion transpired.

So, when we go to any kind of a ceremony—a Pipe ceremony, a Pipefast, a Sundance, wedding, funeral, naming ceremony, or whatever—we should first go into a sweat lodge to purify our mind, our emotions, our spirit, and our physical being, to be able to stand barefooted in a sacred area, fill our Pipes, and pray to the Great Spirit, and we will be certain that He will be there. We will be certain that He will bless us, that He will hear us, that whatever we ask of Him may come to pass.

TALKING TO THE HOLY STONES

by Zintkala Oyate

The healer fills the *Sacred* Pipe. He beckons towards the west, north, east, south, to the heavens, then to our nourishing Mother Earth. All the while the Pipe filling song is sung.

The medicine man enters the ancient spiritual world of this sacred rite. Here we cleanse our impurities, heal our age-old wounds, and begin to grow, love, and forgive. He enters uttering a simple *mitakuye oyasin* (for all my relations). We do the same as we follow him in.

The healer motions and *Tunkas* (the Grandfathers) are brought in and set in the west, then the north, east, and south, toward the heavens, and finally our Mother Earth which he sprinkles with the essence of cedar. The final, and seventh, Grandfather (*Tunka*) is to help us help ourselves.

SACRED FIREPLACE

The water is brought in and all of us grip the rim of the container. The healer invokes the blessing from ancient oral tradition. We acknowledge and submit to its sacredness. The time has come, the time is now, it has begun. In spirit and in prayer we have begun as one.

The door is closed. Although there are many in this sacred place, each one of us is alone. A four directional song is sung with the medicine man in the lead. Someone is beating a drum; it helps. Water is poured on the *Tunkas*; the steam is everywhere.

The spirit-calling song is sung with respectful love. The person sitting across from the healer begins his prayer. We support his prayer and feel his need and we give it hope. Individual prayers continue in a clockwise direction, each ending with "*Mitakuye oyasin.*" The space in the holy wheel of prayer has come to me.

"Great Mystery, Grandfather, look this way. There is nothing holy in and around this place, only that which You have touched and it becomes holy. I send my voice, its pleas spoken from my heart, and it is my spirit's choice.

"I know from the concourses of the avenue of light that through the Grandfathers You can hear my thoughts. My love for You is here, and I have no doubts. In doing so You have made the words of this prayer holy.

"This plea is to ensure that I do not forget we are all related, that I am here as part of Your perfect design, that the path I will follow is of love and growth. I admit and acknowledge that I sometimes

CEREMONIES

become weak and succumb to vices that are virtueless and thus harm myself more.

"It is then that I crawl here to find out what has gone wrong and You are always here. I love You, Great Spirit, *Mitakuye oyasin*."

There are a few more prayers, and a couple more songs are sung. The healer says the word for the door to open. As the door opens, the hot air rushes out and cool air slowly comes in. We all sit silently in sincere reverence. This is how the generations before us have acted, listening to the sounds coming from the Grandfathers. It is said, and I believe that any individual who is prepared and understands can hear the Grandfathers talking, that he or she can hear the old songs that become new as if reborn.

The medicine man looks at every individual to see and feel if anything is wrong. He has the power to let you continue or release you from this prayer. He finds that all is one and he motions for the door to close a second time.

The healer is praying in the ancient language. We are not listening, because we are singing the song of compassion, the song of love, and the song of unity. There is an upsurge of emotional energy expanding outward in me. There is no fear in me now; I do not understand the word. The intense heat numbs my senses and it's as if I am a song, a song building my love for *Wakan Tanka*. I am joy, I am happy, I am someone. The medicine man shouts "*Mitakuye oyasi!*" and the door opens.

SACRED FIREPLACE

There is a long silence. You can hear the breaths of relief as normal air replaces the hot, steamy moisture of this spiritual place in this sacred rite.

When the medicine man motions, the doorman walks to the fire to retrieve a small dry limb that has been placed there for this purpose. He takes the bowl of the *Sacred* Pipe in his left hand and kneels in the doorway. He begins to puff on the Pipe with the burning limb stationed above the rim of the bowl. The *cansasa* (or *kinnikinnick - Algonquin word*) ignites and smoke comes.

The Pipe journeys from person to person, received from the right and passed to the left. It comes to me, I clasp it with firm hands and gently puff from the stem. I repeat what is in my heart. The smoke enters my body as an incense to clear the cocoon of my spirit, to open the wings of my prayer, the words of my love spiraling forth in purity. I pass it on by saying, "*Mitakuye oyasin.*"

The medicine man finishes the *Sacred* Pipe and sends it out. He motions to the doorman as he fills the dipper with the blessed water. It is now medicine for the spirit and the doorman takes a sip and passes it on in the same manner as the Pipe; not one drop is spilled.

The motion is made and the door is closed for the third time. The healer says, "I do not speak in English in this sacred place. Those of you who speak our ancient language know what has transspired in the first two rounds, that we are here in our journey to the center of this beautiful prayer. We have cried together, prayed together, sung together, and watered the flower of our growth in understanding. For life to continue, it must embrace

CEREMONIES

that love in your heart, to know that you have gained a treasure you alone know to be true. Now I return to my language."

There are three ending songs and all of us shout "Mitakuye oyasin!" and the door is opened. There is a long silence. I feel a tingling all over my body. I still feel the presence of the spirits, the helpers of this Spotted Eagle medicine man. I have gained understanding of my burdens so that I can deal with them differently, now that I know I am not alone.

The door is closed for the last time. The healer's spirit helpers have left and we cleanse ourselves for the last time. All of us get ready to re-enter the realm of the living. The blessed water is returned to the Grandfathers and we are happy. I feel joy of life and I shout the songs in echoing gaiety, for my love of the Great Spirit will never end. From my heart I send this thanksgiving song:

Wakan Tanka wopila ecece ye ye lo
Wakan Tanka wopila ecece ye ye lo
Wakan Tanka wopila ecece ye lo hey ho
Cannunpa wan yuha wacece la
unko amayalupta ca pilamaya ya ya lo
Wakan Tanka wopila ecec ye lo hey.
Mitakuye Oyasin.

Great Mystery, I thank you
Great Mystery, I thank you

SACRED FIREPLACE

> *Great Mystery, I thank you*
> *With this Sacred Pipe, I have asked you*
> *and you have answered; I thank you*
> *Great Mystery, I thank you*
> *For all my relations.*

The door opens, and we leave.

HANBLECEYA **(PIPEFAST)**

The Pipe Way is the pathway of this sacred Red Road of Life. Without it, we cannot walk the sacred Red Road of Life. It has a talk of its own, the *Canupa Tawooglake*. I cannot translate that,

CEREMONIES

because when you translate it, it is all wrong. That is why when you pray with the Pipe, you have to talk Lakota, pray Lakota, because the English language can mean so many different things. English is a deceptive language. They (the spirits) hear it this way, but the man that is saying it could mean an altogether different thing. The Lakota language is true and it does not have curse words. The only bad word in the Lakota language is the word "bad."

Hanbleceya, or the Pipefast. It is one of the sacred rites given to our people, and it is a prayer that, to me, is a most beautiful prayer. It is unique, and apart from the rest, even though all the other sacred rites given to us are beautiful. I think the Pipefast, the *Hanbleceya*, is truly the way I would pray to the Great Spirit, because no one is there to hear you. You stand out there in the heat of the day, wherever the selected place is, and pray for, say, one day and one night, or two days and two nights, or three days and three nights, or the whole four days and four nights. You cannot go beyond four days and four nights.

There is an Indian saying that whatever you do, do with your heart in it. If you exceed that, there is such a thing as overdoing it. Then there is such a thing as not doing enough. We have to keep that in mind.

When we say a pledge to go through a Pipefast, we are not saying things that we can change later on. If we say we are going to go on a Pipefast for four days and four nights, we must under no circumstances change the number of days. We have to go four days and four nights, because

SACRED FIREPLACE

regardless of who you are - king, queen, president of the United States - you should not tell the Great Spirit that they will do something one way and then slack off, or do it another way. When you talk to the Great Spirit on selection of a day, you have to do exactly what you have told Him; otherwise, the Pipefast is nothing at all, it is just wasted time. It is crucial for the Pipefast to be precise, even if one has to go through the heat of the day, the cold of the night, the wind, the rain, the hail, whatever else; you have to go through with it.

In preparing for a Pipefast, you have to do certain things. First, you have to prepare your Pipe. In the old Indian world, when people wanted to go on a fast, they prepared their own Pipes with their own hands. They did not go to a museum, or an arts and crafts store, and buy a Pipe that is already made. I will tell you why. Do you know who made that Pipe? Do you know the history? Maybe it was a drunk who commercializes Pipes and is just selling them to buy more alcohol. Maybe that kind of person made the Pipe that you may have bought. You have to be very, very careful because you will be going into the presence of the Great Spirit.

You have to be vitally certain to do things right, and do it with your heart in the doing. In the old days, they had to fashion their Pipe from the Pipe stone. They had to seek and acquire from somewhere, a chunk of Pipe stone, and they would fashion it. They did not sit there day and night until it was done. They worked on it, and they set it aside and did the other chores that needed to be done, chopping wood, looking for horses, cutting hay, putting up hay, repairing a root cellar, or

CEREMONIES

whatever the need in the daily life of the Indian. When I say looking for horses, I talk of the Indian world fifty or sixty years ago.

Sometimes at night when the family is quiet - when the children and the man's wife have all gone to sleep - then he would sit alone and get to fashioning that Pipe stone. When he has fashioned the stone, he would wait until the middle of winter to get the Pipe stem because any other time of the year, it is going to crack. In the middle of the winter, all the sap that is in a tree drains into the ground, so there is less chance of a piece of wood cracking.

Long ago the Pipefast was seen as a fearful thing. It is not something that young bucks today like to do. Without preparing, they buy a Pipe somewhere or even borrow one somewhere. The Pipe that you use is supposed to be yours, and you have to fashion it with loving care. It has to become a part of you.

You would also need a pail, a knife, a wooden bowl, a buffalo skull, and if possible, you would need some sweet grass. You have to have *cansasa* (Indian tobacco), not the kind that you buy, not the kind that is in a plastic bag. You have to fashion it yourself by going out into the canyons and along the creeks, gathering the *cansasa* (the inner bark of the red willow) and make your own *cansasa* tobacco. You gather it before the first lightening happens in the Spring. You dry it, crumble it, and then add that medicine that goes with it.

The rest of the things needed for a Pipefast are flags for the Four Directions, a tobacco tie fence to enclose the area where the person is to fast, four little red flags representing the four virtues, and a

SACRED FIREPLACE

sleeping bag. In the old Indian world a man would take a buffalo robe with him on a Pipefast. Nowadays, they take a sleeping bag, star quilt, what you need to stay warm, which I approve of, because a person needs to sleep. In sleeping a person may receive answers to his prayers. In sleeping, he may dream a sacred dream.

The preparation to fashion the Pipe that he is to pray with and getting together the other things that he needs to have would perhaps take him three months. In the meantime, he would speak to a medicine man, the one of his choice, to help him. The medicine man would advise him on certain things and what to do.

When you have everything ready, the greatest thing in preparation is yourself. One year's time, that is usually the preparation time. If you are prone to anger, you have to throw that out. If you always have bad thoughts of others or if you womanize, get these behaviors out of your system. If money has you by the nose and leads you on, get that out of your system. I know a lot of young men and women are junkies, on alcohol, on *peji* (marijuana) and drugs. These people that I mentioned will require not one year of preparation, but two years of preparation to get that junk out of your system, and then you can go on a Pipefast.

You must get your inside prepared because you are going to pray to the Great Spirit. When all is in readiness, you pray with these things that you have made ready, and you put them away with loving care. You take care of them until the proper time when you are ready to go on a Pipefast.

CEREMONIES

Again always remember that you must do whatever you told the Great Spirit you would do. If you say you were going to go two days and two nights, never change that. Do not get caught up and say that you will go four days and four nights, because you already told the Great Spirit that you will only go two days and two nights, or whatever amount of days and nights that you had mentioned. You may fool yourself, you may fool your fellow man, you may even try to fool the medicine man, but you can never, ever fool the Great Spirit. We cannot play around with Him because I will tell you why. If you change your days, if you told the Great Spirit what you would do and then change it, how do you expect Him to answer you when you pray to Him? You fooled around with Him, so He in turn, will fool around with you. It is as simple as that.

Through the years that I have helped young people men and women go on a Pipefast, I have seen all kinds of weather. I even had one that I placed in the Rosebud country that he went three days and three nights, and all the time he was out there it was raining. So what do you think, what does the medicine man do? Is there some mistake why it is this way? It is a good question. You had better ask yourself, because I do not know.

I can only say that you should remember that whatever you are out there seeking, the elements that *Wakan Tanka* controls will make it worthwhile. If it rains all the way through, if on your second day a hailstorm comes, it is not for you to run from that sacred area (which a lot of people have done). Take it. You have the necessary ability in your mind to overcome the problem that wants to wrest you away from that sacred area. If you believe in this

SACRED FIREPLACE

Wakan Tanka, come hail or high water, you will remain there and pray to Him.

On one occasion I had my sister on a fast. She was sitting in a sweat lodge because she was blind. We had a heck of a rainstorm that night and she was sitting in a flowing stream of water, halfway up to her armpits. So you can imagine, you have a wonderful mind that Wakan Tanka gave you, you think ahead and ask yourself, what will my days and nights present themselves as—punishment for my life, the way I lived?

The Indian prayer in the Pipe Way was very unique. This is what I mean by unique, it stands on its own, and is not like other religions. I remember years and years ago when I used to drink, I used to go to church with a terrible hangover. But here, in this Lakota prayer, you cannot do that. You have to be honest with yourself, you have to clean your system because *Wakan Tanka* will be present where you will go.

I know of one young lady that went on a Pipefast for three days and three nights. She was sitting in a sweat lodge. Every time I approached her, every time I went to check on her, she would be crying. I said nothing, I just noticed that she was crying. Afterwards she told me, "I looked at my life. I reviewed my life and asked myself, why am I sitting here?" I told her it was a good beginning, that she admitted in the presence of the Great Spirit how wrong her former life was, that *Wakan Tanka* loves her, that He blessed her, that she should continue on and acquire a Pipe and become a Pipe carrier. Her former life is done, it is over. A new life has begun, a lovely, beautiful way of life has begun.

CEREMONIES

She is still in that way. She leads sweat lodge ceremonies, she does the praying, she does the singing. *Hanbleceya*, as we know, is so beautiful, so strong, so lovely.

Let me tell you a story about *Hanbleceya* in that other Indian world. Earlier in this century in 1906, there was a young man who had a sacred dream and wanted to go on a Pipefast. He went to a medicine man and talked of his dream, and he asked this medicine man, "When can I present you with a Pipe to help me go through with this plan of *Hanbleceya*?" The medicine man said, "Anytime you feel like it, I will be willing to help you."

He went home and was talking to his father about it and his father said, "I will loan you my Pipe so that you can go and offer him the Pipe to help you. After you come back you will have to fashion your own Pipe - the stone and the stem. You will have to get the things necessary together. You ask him what you need to have and he will tell you. Most of all, you take care of yourself. Clean yourself, make yourself good so that when you pray the *Hanbleceya*, the Great Spirit will listen to you."

In the ensuing months, the young man was lucky. He acquired a piece of Pipe stone. In the evenings he worked on it, fashioning the Pipe stone into the bowl. That winter he went out, and got a stem, and fashioned that, too. He got the other things together, and so, by the time spring came around he was all ready. He had prepared himself as well and he went to several sweat lodge ceremonies.

They selected a day and he went on the fast. They put him out on the plains on the side of a hill. It is a sad story because he did not make it. He

SACRED FIREPLACE

came back the very first night and he was sorry, he was sad. But, he said, "I will try again." So the following summer he tried again. They placed him at a different place and he came back again, he did not make it again. The third time they placed him in another place and, once again he did not make it. That is three times that he failed to finish a Pipefast.

Now, this is a real story I am telling you. You see, young men nowadays that go on a fast would say, "Aw, shucks, it is nothing," because they did not have a sacred dream. Since he failed three times, his father advised him, "Go to that other medicine man. He is very strict. Explain the situation, that you ran from the sacred area three times. Tell him that you want to be guided under him." He wanted to make sure, make certain that he would go through this time because this was the final effort. If he failed in this one, there is no more trying.

It is that important, the Indian prayer comes once. If you fail the four times, it is not meant for you to continue. You have your answer there. Anyway, he went to this strong medicine man and told him the situation, about his sacred dream, and that he tried to go on a fast for three summers in a row, and every time he ran from the place. He said then, "I want you to do all you can to keep me there so that I would not be able to come away." So the medicine man accepted his Pipe, and he said, "I will."

The day arrived for the final try of a fast. The medicine man rode a horse. The young man going on the fast rode another horse that dragged a travois carrying all the necessary things. The

CEREMONIES

medicine man took a stake as tall as his shoulder and a heavy maul. Then he took him way out and placed him in a special place, he knocked this stake into the ground clear to the tip of it, and he notched it. He took wet rawhide and wrapped it several times around the stake and tied it with sinew. Then he took his knife and pierced the young man's chest very deep. He had let the wet rawhide dry so it was pointed and stiff like a pencil. When he pierced him, he put the rawhide through and pulled it way out and tied it with wet sinew so it would not come out. He said, "This will keep you here." Blood was streaming down. He chewed some medicine and put it on the cut to stop the flow. Then he left him.

When the medicine man came back to camp, he stopped on a hill and looked back. The medicine man was hurt - never before had he experienced a situation in like this and he was heavyhearted. He kept standing there watching him, until the sun set. He did that for two purposes: to see how the young man was reacting to the way that he was placed in the situation; and he wanted the rawhide that was soaked and limber, to dry up, and the wet sinew that was tied on the ends to dry up.

When the sun set, the medicine man walked his horse home. At the evening meal he told his wife and two sons, "Go ahead and eat. I feel very deeply for the young man that I took out there. He is constantly in pain and he will be there for three days and three nights and I am wondering, wondering how he will fare. So, my family, go ahead and eat. My concern is for him and I will fast along with him. I will smoke my Pipe and stay awake. I won't even lie down; I will sit in a chair and

SACRED FIREPLACE

wait for daybreak to get here to help him in his prayer."

He was sitting there, hour upon hour, and towards daybreak, the Lakota people have a word, *ehake eyokpaza,* which means the last dark portion of the night before the first light of dawn. About that time over in the back there was something heavy that hit the ground. The medicine man thought that it was a neck yoke - the front piece of a wagon, and then it sounded as if someone slammed it against the outside wall. He got up and woke his two sons and told them, "Get up, there is something heavy that hit the back wall. Let us go out and check." They lit a lantern—in those days there were no flashlights. They went out and shone this light on the outside back wall of the house. There laid the young man. The pierced thong was still intact. All the length of that rawhide was still unbroken and the long heavy piece of timber that he knocked into the earth to tie him to had been pulled out and lying there. The young man was unconscious.

They took a knife and cut his breast where the piercing was done. They cut the rawhide away, carried him inside, and placed him on a bed. They wet his face, fanned him, and he came to. He looked about. He did not know where he was. The medicine man told him, "They (the spirits) brought you back."

The young man said he was standing there, really tired, and he wanted to sit down. When he sat down the area changed to white, to red, to green, to yellow, and then it changed to darkness; that is all he knew.

CEREMONIES

In the evening they went into a Pipe ceremony to find out why this happened, a young man trying four consecutive times to finish a fast and was unable to do so. The spirits told the medicine man that the young man had a sacred dream and he left out a portion of that sacred dream. He should have told all of it.

When you pray to the Great Spirit, every word that you say must be meaningful. Sacred dreams are that way. If you omit a portion of it, then it is nothing. When I had my sacred vision of getting two handfuls of hot coals in my hand, I knew that was dangerous. I knew that could cause me to lose my hands; I knew there could be hurt and pain. I knew this. Common sense told me that I could be crippled for life. But the belief, the acceptance of a vision, the belief that goes into it, if a person has that, it will be fulfilled.

When a person wants to go on a fast, the preparation has to be real; it has to be clear, precise, and true in form, not jumping into something without preparing. If you do that, it is not a fast. The preparation is most important; it has to be done. Some will say, "No, you do not have to; you just get prepared today and go on a fast tomorrow." This is bullshit. If there is something that is bullshit - it is the kinds of things that false medicine men tell the people, which carries a message that is absolutely wrong.

There are many fakers across this land of ours, as well as the ministers on TV that we hear so much about. You will know a medicine man. You will not find him in a crowd; you will not find him in a pow-wow or a great gathering unless he is invited

SACRED FIREPLACE

there.[9] A fake medicine man attending a great pow-wow will say he was invited there. Oh, these guys just give me a pain in the neck. These guys are fly-by-night; they are nothing. I know a lot of them. I can mention names, but I won't. And in doing so, *Wakan Tanka* loves me all the more.

So, I see the difference in our world today and how different the people lived in the old Indian world many years ago. No wonder the Great Spirit loves the Lakota people - they did it right, they did it straight, and they prayed in the Lakota language.

"*Tunkasila, Wakan Tanka, onsimilaye ikca wicasa onsiamakaagic. Mi takuye yoti wakinyan. Ikca wicasa ta cannunpa yuha. Hoye ciciye.*" This is the way we should pray.

---

[9] A genuine medicine man attends a pow-wow or other gathering only when invited by the organizers to "say the main prayer." The medicine man may then remain on site until the end of the pow-wow to retrieve eagle feathers that may fall to the ground, thereby preventing harm to the participants.

CEREMONIES

Hanbleceya **(Pipefast)**

WITHIN THE UNSEEN REALM

by Zintkala Oyate

I have come here for the past two years. This is my third fast with my Pipe. It is in the middle of the night of the third day. I have seen two sunrises and two sunsets, my inner self crying painful tears. This is the Spotted Eagle Way.

My father came here, as did his father before him; generations after generation the line continued as that of the first thought. This is the Pipe Way. You find peace in your heart and there is also fear.

SACRED FIREPLACE

Its genesis is the sacred hoop, which has no begining and no end.

I look skyward, and see the twinkling stars. I hear a rumbling and I know it is within me. I am hungry. I recall earlier in the hot day how thirsty I was, how my thoughts were hard to concentrate on prayer because of that physical thirst.

It is these physical barriers that haunt me now in the cold of the night. I clasp my Pipe harder and pray harder. It is my devotion, my personal path, and not like those of others before or after me. I know I am not alone in this unique prayer of fasting. I have become part of a universal creation, and know only that my spirit is growing. I know I have become a spiritual explorer to gain knowledge of peaceful acceptance of life, of being a part of it, and knowing that it is sacred.

Memories in turn are another form of my mental and emotional growth. Except that I now look towards my future from this present place, always with hope and knowing that the Great Mystery is here with me now, encouraging my love of others and that I am special. I turn slowly in a clockwise motion until I face the west and sit down slowly, cross legged, and tap into the umbilical cord of the Earth, my Mother. My physical presence is drained away, immediately replaced by a life energy with an awesome riveting beat, yet mildly flowing. I realize then that I have achieved another level in my spiritual journey.

"*Wakan Tanka, Tunkasila*, I pray to you as I stand up and turn to face the place where the dawn's light hides the stars and the morning star twinkles its last message to my heart. This heart of mine will always

CEREMONIES

remain a doorway to that enlightened message. Great Mystery, your mysterious movement ignites a fire of love not ever wanting in my soul."

I hear the shrill of an eagle far away; it is getting closer. Then I feel that I am lying down. The sun is hot. I slowly sit up with my Pipe. I am somewhat bewildered. Then I remember, and I look around me and I see the green, red, yellow, and gray tobacco flags, the tobacco tie fence, and the altar. Everything is as it should be.

I see that I must have slept most of the bright day. I stand up to see the medicine man and his helpers coming slowly. Upon arrival, he smudges the area with sweetgrass. Oblivious to me, he prays and then sings a song. The medicine man is followed by the one who carries the buffalo skull altar. No words are said; everyone is quiet.

The fire at the *initi* has been burning throughout the time that I was fasting with my Pipe. The medicine man motions for me to go into the *initi* and sit in the back, opposite the door. He sits down to the right of the door opening and one of his helpers sits opposite him. Seven *Tunkas* are brought in one at a time, and then the living water is brought in and he prays with it and motions for the door to close. How I remember the eighth *Tunka*. I remember the day I came upon the stone and as clear memories held me, I had a particular fear - of the unknown in my quest, of loving the Great Mystery. I touched every little indentation in the stone, slowly and carefully picked this rock that I will know forever, and felt it to ask it if it would help me someday. In my heart, I knew this was the humble way in which

SACRED FIREPLACE

one should ask to be a part of the love and the key to its design.

I remember the other fasts. Now I more clearly see through the clouds of the darkened sky. I remember the eighth *Tunka* to help me come back anew. The first seven cleaned me and helped me here, that I might recognize the road and step slowly without fear in this path of virtue so lovingly handed down from our ancestors, guided by the Goddess of Harmony, that no thought can grasp Her beauty. Now I feel revived to live some more.

In the times I have come here, I have been shown that I am loved by an incomprehensible force which gave me this gift of love. The door is opened; the medicine man's helper takes sage and wipes my forehead, hands, and feet. The medicine man prays with a bowl of water and cherry juice to give to me to break my fast; it is bitterly wonderful. I am happy. The door closes. We sing together. Another door has opened, and we leave. *Mitakuye oyasin.*

CEREMONIES

Petaga Yuha Mani praying during Sundance

WIWANGYANG WACIPI (SUNDANCE)

I would like to talk about the Sundance and the proper way to go through with the ritual of a Sundance. There are many versions, especially, shall we say, up-to-date versions. I think that early writers who wrote about Sundances put too much "butter" on the thing. Young people of today get the

SACRED FIREPLACE

notion that a Sundance has to be cruel, in regards to torture and suffering, as it was depicted years ago. A Sundance does not always entail the piercing of the flesh. It does not have to. A Sundancer can dance four full days without getting pierced and still be able to achieve his goals.

So powerful is that ritual when people do not abuse it. I use the word "abuse," because young bucks today have a tendency to abuse the sacred rituals that were given to us, even the sweat lodge. A person can abuse that by making it too hot, so too with the Sundance. We do not hang Sundancers on the pole; I have never seen it, but I have heard that in some places the dancers were hung in mid-air alongside the Sundance Tree. The Tree is sacred; we only put prayer flags or prayer offerings on the Tree.

When we go to a Sundance, we take in the whole picture. You see the crowd; there is always a big crowd. We have planned for the Sundance to take care of all of the people's needs throughout the ceremony. At one side off at a distance is the cook shack where food is prepared for the elderly, the sick, babies, young people, those that do require food at the Sundance. Near the cook shack area also is the water that the spectators may drink, because children, old people, sickly people, elderly people need water. We build shaded camping areas and outhouses that will accommodate the people that go there and camp. Then, in the immediate area underneath the arbor where the crowd will gather, you have sick people sitting here and there. To the south of the arbor, where the white flags are, the drummers and singers are seated.

CEREMONIES

The Sundance Tree represents many things. First of all, it stands as a cane to lean upon, to grow with, to hang onto. If it is a very hot day, you can sit in the shade of the Sundance Tree. I have seen this done very often. The Sundance Tree is commonly called the Tree of Life, because it does give life. It corrects our health problems, gives us a new lease on life. So, to dance the Sundance properly, one need not pierce his flesh. Dancing for four days, abstaining from food and drink is suffering enough. Four days of fasting to purge ourselves from the impurities that have come into our life is enough.

The day before "Tree Day," when we put the tree up, the scouts go out to search and select the tree. (They do not have to be scouts nowadays because we do not really live in the realm of the old world and the old Indian ways. But we call them scouts anyway). The Sundance tree could be several miles away. On "Tree Day" everyone - the campers, the dancers, or whoever is present at the time - are privileged to go along, so a stream of cars goes out where the Sundance tree is. The medicine man clears a place beneath the Sundance tree and scatters some sage and he lets his Pipe rest there.

On occasion, the medicine man will talk to the crowd, explaining what is being done, because many of the people that have come to a Sundance for the first time will not understand what is taking place. He will tell why they are doing this. Four young girls are selected, and they are prettied up with deerskin and eagle feathers or whatever the family can afford, and they stand in readiness to perform the tree chopping ceremony. After the medicine man talks a bit about what is going to

SACRED FIREPLACE

happen and its meaning, he goes into the filling of his Pipe.

I will focus on how I usually conduct a Sundance. Our presence there and all of our work involved in the Sundance, whether we pray or not, indicates that we are part of the Sundance prayer. I cannot tell all that goes through the mind of a Sundancer, because they are all individual. But, in my mind, I know what goes on. I cannot tell you everything that goes on, you have to be there to see or to hear what takes place at a Sundance. What I am telling you here is what we do at our Sundance, not the one in Rosebud, not the one elsewhere. They do it differently and they would talk about it differently, but the Sundance I am talking about happens at our place called *Pte Woku* [Feeding the Buffalo], an old residence of ours. Our children grew up there. It is a nice location. It is like a table that has a lot of camping area. But it is a dry camp. We need a well there because we do this annually and we have to haul our water.

When I start filling my Pipe for the four days of the coming Sundance, the drummer will be singing the Pipe filling song invoking the Four Directions and their God-given power. This, so that the people will live, that the coming generations will grow up and be plentiful, and that health and good will be among the people, to take care of the elderly, and whatever our cares are at the time. Many times, we think about soldier boys during the war years, World War II, the Korean Conflict, Vietnam. In those times, we audibly say prayers for the soldier boys. We never forget the sick who are in the hospitals, or those that are in prison, and those relatives that are not with us now that have gone beyond the great divide. A red cloth flag with tobacco pouch is tied to the tree, and red paint is smeared at the base of the tree. All these signify the intentions of the people. All are in union at that moment beneath the Sundance tree.

When the Pipe filling is done, we go into the Four Directions song using the drum. My older son stands on one side of me, my youngest son stands on the other side, and we begin singing the songs to the Four Directions, to the heavens above, to the earth below. When this is done a medicine man directs the young maidens who are to chop the tree, to give it one blow. He has instructed them how to do it, and he has told them why they were selected, that it is an honorable place, an honorable occasion, just like giving a person a name. He tells them that fifty years hence, when they have grown up to be old ladies with children and grandchildren, each one should be able to tell her children and grandchildren, that one time in her life she came upon a chosen time which was honorable. She was selected to give the one chop of the hatchet to the sacred tree.

Each of the four girls takes a position in one of the four directions beneath the Sundance Tree that is going to be cut down. According to instructions by the medicine man, the one to the west brings the hatchet and hits the tree at the base, at which time the crowd hollers what we call *akisa (*white people call it a war whoop). The hollering out is invoking a blessing upon those that voice this hollering out. Next in line is the young girl to the north, followed by the one to the east, and last, but not least, the one to the south.

SACRED FIREPLACE

The prayer at one place goes something like this, "Great Spirit, you have planted with your hand this tree at this particular place. The people have come from the center of the hoop and selected this tree that you planted here. They decorated it with a red flag and painted it red, signifying the race of people that you, the Divine Being, created. And in your inspiration, the people have at this time brought four maidens, very innocent in life, to give the first chop with the hatchet in the Four Directions, directions that you made sacred and holy, that henceforth where this Tree goes will be a holy and sacred place."

Next the men, the workers who are helping to make this Sundance a reality, will take an axe and start chopping down the Tree. They guide the Tree to fall one way and some stand on that side with long branch forks, sticks, and poles that are maybe ten or twelve feet long to catch the falling tree with the crutch at the end of the pole, because we know that when the tree falls, it should not touch the ground. Women always have a place in our sacred ceremonies. Some, if it is feasible, lay their shawls and blankets along the way where the tree will fall; that way the branches and the leaves will not touch the earth. When they cut down the Sundance Tree, no part of it should touch the ground. The thing about this is that the Great Spirit planted this tree here. He let it grow to this height, to this size, and the people came from within the sacred hoop to claim it, to take it from this place where it was planted to take it to the center of their sacred hoop and replant it there to become the Sundance Tree.

Of course, because we are human, and there being the elements all around us, whether it is wind or

CEREMONIES

whatever, some of the branches may touch the ground. These branches will be cut. Some do it right there, but in our case we just mark it and cut them when we take it back to the center of the sacred hoop. By sacred hoop, I mean the arbor where the Sundance is to be held.

We have a volunteer to move the tree. We place it in a pickup with young men holding on to it, standing in the box, or riding on the hood and hanging on so it will not fall off. One year we even carried it on top of a van. We come back to the Sundance grounds in a procession with a filled Pipe taking the lead. When we arrive at a distance that we have agreed on, we stop the vehicles and unload the tree there, and from there we carry it. The Sundancers and those that are able to carry the tree on their shoulders take it to the east entrance of the arbor.

On the way to that entrance, we stop four times. At the first stop, I pray and then take them on to the second stop. I have instructed them that at the third stop they should yell all out and give the coyote howl. We stop the third time. Everyone gives the coyote howl and I pray again. The fourth time we stop, we stop at the center of the sacred hoop, the center of the arbor where the Sundance will be held. In the center of the sacred hoop, a hole has been dug in the ground. The Sundance tree will be placed into this hole. The women come forward with their shawls and blankets and lay them on the ground. The Sundance tree is laid on the ground before rising to its final place in the center. It is laid on the ground because it is a lengthy ceremony. We trim the tree at this point, cutting off the limbs that have touched the ground. We trim it up to the

SACRED FIREPLACE

fork. The fork of the Sundance tree is a story in itself, which I will come to later.

I then perform a ceremony and ask the Great Spirit to bless the offerings of tobacco, water, *wasna* (ground dried meat), and buffalo blood. I offer the tobacco to the spirits that have passed on to the Great Divide since the last Sundance. Water is sprinkled in the hole and is likewise offered to the spirits that have left us - our relatives, close friends, or whoever we have in mind. The *wasna*, too, is given to those spirits so that they can feed on it. They in turn will assist us to have a good Sundance. Each of these medicines are offered to the Four Winds, praying all the while to *Wakan Tanka* to bless what is being offered.

When this portion of the ceremony is over, we select one person to take buffalo blood and wet the base of the Sundance tree. When that is done, a cherry tree bundle, along with the offerings for this coming year, are placed in the crutch of the tree and tied securely. This represents the nest of creation. Then the buffalo effigy and the man effigy are tied towards the top. Then a very long red tobacco flag called *waluta,* which represents the Red Road of Life, is tied towards the top. Then those Sundancers who will pierce tie their ropes to the Tree.

When that portion of the ceremony is completed, we hoist the Sundance Tree to a standing position. When it stands full scale in the hole, everybody, including children, grownups, and old people give a yell rejoicing that a new life has begun, that we have entered into another phase of our life. When the Sundance Tree is tamped in solidly, then the

CEREMONIES

ropes that were loose are gathered together and tied at the base. The singers then go into a song. They sing a song they call *Owanka Nasto*. I would not attempt to try to translate the meaning of this song; it is too far beyond me.

Sometimes when I talk like this, the proper words cannot be interpreted. I cannot do it. The Indian language is so different. We sometimes try. I, myself, knowingly try to interpret what we are trying to say, but I know for a certainty that my interpretation is wrong. It does not touch base. It does not say what is said in Lakota. I would not let another language say things that are not worthy of the language that we speak.

During the singing of *Owanka Nasto,* everybody present dances - children, even sick people, and especially in the old days, warriors. They dance at random, between the arbor area where the spectators will sit and the Sundance Tree, which is in the center. It is a lengthy song. You have to make four complete rounds if you are a part of this dancing. You go around the inside of the arbor four times. When that is done, they sing another song. It is a rejoicing song. It is a happy occasion. It is an acceptance song, and people are glad. You see smiles on faces of people knowing that they have witnessed another beginning of another span of one year, they have started a new year. So, it is a time of rejoicing. Everybody is happy.

Right after that, food is brought out and everyone sits in a circle. Many times Lakota people sit in a circle. I remember as a young boy, I saw old people sitting in a circle smoking the *Sacred* Pipe. In those days, they carried a family Pipe, which they

SACRED FIREPLACE

cherished and regarded as very sacred. They handled it with reverence because it was sacred. Back to this Tree ceremony, everyone is sitting in a wide circle. Young people volunteer to distribute food. We have Kool-Aid for children, coffee and tea for the adults; we have meat and soup; we have *wojapi* (berry pudding), fry bread. It is a happy occasion. We enjoy the food of life, food that will be with us through the coming year.

At this point the dancers are still with the people. This is the last food and drink they will partake. Right after the feasting is over, the dancers go off to the sequestered area. They go into the sweat lodge. This is the last time we will talk to them until after the Sundance, because they are kept in this secluded area. No one goes there except the person in charge and myself. No one else goes near them. That is the true way of the Sundance. You do not allow people to come and talk to them. In order to have a good Sundance, you have to step on toes; you have to be a leader. You have to have your rules obeyed. Sometimes you even have to get angry. That is the role of a leader.

When the Sundancers are finished with the Purification Rite, they go into a teepee which is provided for them in the secluded area. But some prefer to sleep under the arbor. A section of the arbor is reserved for them (one section for the men and another section for the women). It is fenced in with pine branches and pine limbs so that is where they recline through the coming four days.

The Sundance is a hard prayer. For one thing, you abstain from food and water. The very first day, your throat is dry. On the second day, you have no

CEREMONIES

spittle, your mouth is dry. The third day, your windpipe seems to crack up. The fourth day, you do not know where you are, but you know someone out there in the crowd, or maybe many people are watching you, helping you. The dancing goes on no matter what kind of a day it is. In the past years that I have Sundanced or directed Sundances, a lot of times we danced in the rain or in the heat of a summer day with temperatures sometimes hitting 110 degrees, and it is terrible. The ordeal is so great. Only a Sundancer knows how great it is.

Petaga Yuha Mani with his Pipe at a Sundance in 1968

If you want to do the Sundance, you will have to abstain from food and water. I have seen Sundances at other places. Last summer I went to four of them, some eating food or drinking water in the

SACRED FIREPLACE

evenings. To me, that is abusing a sacred rite. If they are going to do this, they might as well not dance at all because of the respect due the Sundance. If we do not respect ourselves, we should at least try to respect a sacred rite. If we cannot dance the Sundance four days and four nights, abstaining from food and water, we should, in respect, stay away from it. This kind of a person can be a spectator, a drummer, a singer, a committee man, or a worker there, chopping wood and keeping the fire going. There are also many other chores that need to be done at a Sundance.

We have been having an annual Sundance all on our own. Just my family, my two boys, have somehow managed to put on a Sundance. But very recently, for two years now, we have had committees. We have people that we regard as Keepers of the *Sacred* Pipe and they, their families and their children, pledge to be a part of the Sundance sponsors. So the going is lighter now. It is not as tough and hard as it was in our former years. Every year our crowd is getting bigger and bigger.

There again I will say this. In order to do a Sundance, it has to be four days. One cannot dance one day or two days and drop out. No, you have to go four days. A Sundance is a four-day affair, and it has to be without food and water. You have to pray with the Pipe, so you have to pray the Lakota language. So these are things required in the Sundance ceremonies, that we do every year in the month of July.

There are many things that go with the Sundance. Before this, I mentioned the crutch (fork) in the Sundance Tree. Now I will tell you what I know

CEREMONIES

about that crutch in the Sundance Tree. Sometimes you hear people that get involved with astrology - the Tree itself is like astrology. If you look up at the sky at night, some clear night, especially in the summertime, you would see the cluster of stars called the Milky Way. If you study that Milky Way, it looks like the Sundance Tree. Maybe the first Indian that dreamed about the Sundance, who was chosen to understand and talk about the Sundance and its ways and its songs, knew that this Tree resembles the Milky Way.

Legend tells us that our next life, after we leave this world, is like going through the Milky Way, or going up the Sundance Tree, the spirit trail. There is an expanse of space, very much like we see in the heavens. The two stars that you see close by are perhaps millions of miles apart, and yet from our position, it seems to us they nearly touch each other. So it goes in life. When our spirits walk the Spirit Trail, we come to this crutch or fork in the path. And according to legend, an Old Lady sits there and looks at us as we approach. If you do not have *agito* (enlightenment), this Old Lady will point in the direction of that cut off branch, and this spirit will follow that and go to an end where it falls off into space, into nowhere. When the Old Lady sees a person, a spirit approaching, and it has *agito*, she points to the long way, the remaining distance to the top of the Sundance Tree, or to the top of the Milky Way, and the spirit can go on into that eternal reward into that everlasting bliss, heaven, or as we say "The Land of the Winds."

So the Sundance Rite, as given to us, means that we live in this world. But, if we do the Sundance Rite in a correct manner with our heart in it

SACRED FIREPLACE

and dancing the four days, fasting from food and water, we will reach the very top of that Sundance Tree. The very top of that Sundance Tree will bring us everlasting life to be with those loved ones that have gone before us to be happy forever. This is one aspect of the Sundance that I love so much.

During an intermission of a Sundance where I was present, a person who is well known and very prominent - I will not mention his name - went to the sound system and gave a lengthy talk. In the course of his talk, he said, "Catches taught us many things, and when I look at the man Catches, I think that this Sundance arbor is his home. I think he lives here." My experiences in the many Sundances that I have conducted and was a part of show me that the Great Spirit is present in all the things that we do. I hope that some of you that read this book will understand a little about the Sundance at our place, at Pte Woku. And I hope that through this little talk of mine, the Great Spirit will love you and bless you, you and those that you care for.

CEREMONIES

Petaga Yuha Mani Sundancing 1968

THE LONE SUNDANCER

by *Zintkala Oyate*

I sing the songs of my grandfathers, who were medicine men in their respective clans of the Lakota *Oyate*. I am in this Purification Rite that precedes what I am to do, to cleanse my spirit in

SACRED FIREPLACE

order to approach the sacred ground - the circle underneath the Tree of Life.

It is dawn as I prepare myself inside the *Inipi*, the first rite of the people. I tell the *tunkas* (the birth and the aged) of this dream, which has haunted me for what seems like an eternity. Now I am here to shed that pain and feel its entirety.

I have done the *Hanbleceya* (Pipefast) for four consecutive years, yet the vision persists to make me new, in a day that is yet to dawn. I have tried to avoid its essence many years, because of the shame brought upon us by a different people who believe differently.

Now, by the instructions of the medicine man, both of us chant. In the reality of the chant, we steam ourselves before we leave the sacredness of the *Inipi*. It is still dawn, I am taken by two helpers who sew seven *wanble gleska weyaka* (spotted eagle feathers) on my arms, with one in the middle of my back.

The drum to the south begins a rapid, non-uniform beat. We walk slowly from the west, outside the perimeter of the prayer sticks, slowly towards the red tobacco flags to stop and implore the formless *Wakinyan* (Thunder Beings), who are at the West to bless this day. We continue and stop at the North, with its two long red tobacco tie flags, to implore the T*atanka Oyate* (Buffalo Nation), and for them to hear our plea with this *Sacred* Pipe. We continue and stop the third time, to implore the *Wicasa Wan Kaiglaglag* (Radiant Golden Man), who gives us this sacred day. Then, we continue on to east and stop for the last time at the two long yellow tobacco tie flags before we enter the sacred

CEREMONIES

hoop of the Sundance Nation. Here we implore the *Pahan San Oyate* (Gray Swan Nation) to the south to bless this area of prayer in their divine flight.

The medicine man takes me inside the hoop. He walks in a sacred way inside its perimeter toward the two long gray tobacco tie flags and on to the two long green tobacco tie flags, where he fashioned an alter of sage and the buffalo skull. There he slowly places my lone Pipe.

I turn to the right of the sacred Tree of Life to face the glorious dawn. The drum's beat in unison. My thoughts look upon the east; I feel the chill of the morning air. I hear the hush of beauty in my soul. The song of the ancients is in the air; my essence vibrates with its rhythm and my spirit awakens to the words of the song.

Anpetu ki le wakan yelo

Tokahe ya taku wa yelo

Wamble gleska wan le ya kinyan u welo

Anpetu ki le wakan yelo

Tokahe ya taku wa yelo

Anukan san wan le ya kinyan u welo

This is a holy day

I am the first relative of this day

A spotted eagle is saying this as he comes

SACRED FIREPLACE

This day is holy

I am related first to this day

A bald eagle is saying this as he comes flying

The first rays of the sun break in the east and tears flow inside of me. I feel the awe of the moment.

Pete Sundancing 1968

It has been hours; my dancing is like breathing. My perspiration is like another skin, soothing and cooling me. It is then that the medicine man with another helper takes me by both arms and makes a wide clockwise circle in the hoop of the nation. I am

CEREMONIES

slowly laid down under the Tree of Life with my head towards the altar. I close my eyes to feel a sharp pain above my heart and feel myself being lifted to my feet. "*Wakan Tanka* (Great Spirit), pity me," is the song that is sung.

The medicine man and his helper have left the sacred area. I am alone. My thoughts race back in time - the songs take me there. The four great virtues loom in front of me - fidelity, fortitude, courage, and generosity. I slowly make my selfless plea for wisdom on behalf of the entire community. This plea is made to the universal forces, which I understand to be superior to mankind. I have offered this flesh, for I understand that this is the one thing that is mine alone, mine alone to give. I sacrifice myself in this way. I realize that this area in my reality is the entire universe - the sacred Tree of Life has become Wakan Tanka (Great Spirit), my flesh is ignorance, and the skewers in my flesh are the rays of enlightenment that I receive from the Great Spirit.

By enacting my vision, I have offered my sacrifice, clarifying my willingness to accept an attitude of submission, my equality of obligation to those greater things that we know to be superior to ourselves. This obligation of equality I acquiesce to and invite the rest of the people to join in. In this equality members possess equal respect for one another.

In doing this, I am symbolically submitting to the Sundance Nation in what I perceive to be the rightful location in the nest of creation, and providing the means for acquiring equality of respect and trust. I effortlessly push back the borders of my rightful

SACRED FIREPLACE

community into a realm that is beyond simple description. I sundance, with the forces, with the people, the Sundance Nation.

The sun is overhead at its zenith. I am lost no longer, yet the intensity is mystifying for I feel no pain. And though I cry inside, I know that the vision is just beginning. I feel the power in my sacrifice and I am weary. I know there is a power inside of me, giving me what I need to go on, and I feel happiness to have come this far.

The sun is falling rapidly; the ancient songs are enhancing the sacred area of worship. Over toward the west, the Thunder Beings loom as they approach forebodingly. Their shapeless forms rumble and their eyes are spears of searing light. I feel an uneasiness that makes me tremble. They are coming low, stomping the earth. the people are afraid. I know what must be done.

I call for my *Sacred* Pipe and it is given to me. This is the haunting dream, the painful reality. I slowly lift my *Sacred* Pipe toward the thunderhead, close my eyes, and whisper the sacred words from the Land of the Winds. The reality of my sacrifice bounds forth with my faith. It is an inspiration so deep, guided by a just belief, that upon opening my eyes, the thunderhead is parted. And suddenly, in between the parted storm clouds flies the spotted eagle. It is over. The feathers sewn on my arms seem to come alive. Joy unfolds inside my soul; the feeling is of pure ecstasy. The feathers pull me upward and I dance to the rhythm. With outstretched arms and feathers whirling, I run backwards and feel myself break free.

CEREMONIES

This vision, this sacred dream completed, only reveals the Red Road of Life. The path of the Pipe religion of the Sundance *Oyate* is a connection between religion and philosophy, with the practice of good living. It is an inspirational foundation based upon an experiential religion. Everyone becomes a member, and above all, a holy being created by God.

Pete at his home with friend

HUNKAPI (MAKING OF A RELATIVE)

The making of a relative is one of the Seven Sacred Rites given to the Lakota people. I will not go into full detail as to what it really means. But the beginning part of it is that on the anniversary of

SACRED FIREPLACE

losing people we love who have left this world and gone into the Great Hereafter - children, brothers, grandchildren, sisters - we commemorate the occasion with a feast. When we lose a member of our families, we seek solace and comfort. The way the Indian people do this is to make a relative of someone living to replace the one we lost. In this way, the only way to acquire the nearness of those we lost is to make a relation of someone who makes us think of them because of their appearance, disposition, character, or way of life. We tend to bring that person into our family group, to become one of us in the absence of the real one. In our culture, we think that what we do with the adopted one is the same we would do with the one we have lost.

According to this way of thinking and the way of life that Wakan Tanka gave to us, we have this sacred rite. We can make a relationship or a friendship with anyone, and as implied, we have to go through a ceremony. The way to do that is to go through a sweat lodge ceremony to prepare ourserves physically and spiritually with the one that we are to make a relative. In preparing for this ceremony, the women go to beading deer hide moccasins and dresses. There are many types of buckskin dresses with many designs on them. There are also headpieces, front pieces, necklaces and belts. Some of these will be given to people at the give-away part of the ceremony.

When going into the ritual, a white cloth is stretched between two poles, denoting that the loved one has crossed over. The white connotes purity. We, on each side, will come together in

CEREMONIES

purity, resembling this white cloth, in the spirit and physically.

There are certain songs for the occasion and a certain kind of drumbeat. A gourd with an ear of corn mounted on the handle and another stick with horsetail hair hung at the end are shaken in time with the beat of the drum. The people are dancing along throughout, touching both parties during the time the gourd is shaking in time with the drum.

The dancers make a complete circle. The song is repeated four times to the west, and they dance in that direction, to the north and they dance in that direction, to the east and they dance in that direction, and to the south, they, in turn, dance to that direction, making a complete circle.

The two who are united in relationship are touched with the horsetail hair. This requires a certain amount of skill because you have to be able to keep time with the gourd in your left hand. The spectators who watch these ceremonies see the sacredness. Even awkward, slow-moving, unlively people become lively and skillful dancers when handling the gourd and the ear of corn.

The medicine man who conducts the ceremony then gives water and food, praying with it and placing it there. The two becoming related must feed each other. One feeds the new relation, and the new relation feeds the one that fed him. This is unity, a coming together, in prayer, in action, and song, in a physical way and in spirit. Blessed by the Great Spirit, becoming relatives by a sacred rite that begins at that moment, to last forever in this world and on into the next.

SACRED FIREPLACE

When this part of the ceremony is over, we go feast. There is much feasting, all provided by the person who makes a relative of someone. A large crowd is fed, and then there is a giveaway, bundles of articles accumulated over the past year. We like to talk about generosity. If you attend these ceremonies, you will see what generosity entails.

When you go to a restaurant and sit down to a good meal, an exceptionally good meal, you remember it and tell your friends, "That restaurant is a good one. They served me good food and they made me comfortable. I felt at home." So too, in this feasting at the Making of a Relative, there are many kinds of food. The amount of food is so plentiful that everyone is well fed, and parts of the food are taken home. We call it *wateca*, and it is like taking a part of the feast to those at home. There might be a sick person at home unable to attend the gathering; through *wateca*, they are able to partake of some of this feasting food, blessed on the occasion by the Great Spirit.

The Indian people look at food as the number one medicine, the first food that man lives on. We consider food to be medicine because we are sustained by it and we gain strength from it; because we are happy when we are well fed and glad to be alive. We then look at life from another perspective. We are thankful that we can go on with good food in us, making us strong and happy, and this food is carried home.

Many things are given away to visitors, so that when they go home, in the direction of the four points of the compass, they will say, "I received this at that Making of a Relative sacred rite ceremony.

CEREMONIES

They gave much food away, they gave horses away, they gave money away." The tidings are taken home, and people who were not present will know that there are two people who became relatives on that occasion.

I experienced this Making of a Relative twice in my life. Once I was made a little brother to Silas Black Dog of Rosebud country. He is originally from Rosebud, but he married into the Lower Brule tribe, where he lived and passed away. Over in the Rosebud country, at Spring Creek, I was adopted in the Paul Swift Hawk family, so I have relatives there as I speak. I have younger sisters, younger brothers, I have nieces, nephews, and grandchildren living in Spring Creek at this time. My brother Silas Black Dog passed away early in 1970 and my father, Paul Swift Hawk, passed away several years ago.

It is good to note that *Wakan Tanka*, in His goodness, takes care of His people. I do not know what a father is, and I really do not know what a mother is. When I was very young, I lost my father and mother. But, the Great Spirit saw to it that in the life of Paul Swift Hawk, he chose to make me his son. I became his oldest son, because their first-born passed away when the boy was in infancy. And if this boy were alive, my adopted father told me, he would have been exactly my age. A coincidence that I should mention is that my real father's first name is Paul, and my adopted father's first name is also Paul.

My relations in Spring Creek are much cherished and we love one another. I used to spend parts of every summer there. Just recently, I received an

SACRED FIREPLACE

emergency message that the Pine Ridge police delivered to my trailer camp. A younger brother, Ben Swift Hawk, passed away at Spring Creek. My wife and I traveled to Rosebud country and attended the wake and funeral of my brother, Ben, at Spring Creek. At the funeral, I sang a song during the covering of the grave.

Afterward, I dreamed about my little brother, Ben. At first, I did not know it was him. I saw an Indian with long hair in regalia with an eagle feather tied to his head. The horse he was riding was restless, eager to go, high-spirited. When the warrior on this horse moved at a certain angle, I would see certain parts of his cheek; he was wearing war paint. Down in the canyon was a river and, among the trees, I could see thirteen or fourteen buffalo, some were lying down, others were standing in the river, drinking water, and still others were under the trees.

Over to the right, below a sloping hill, was a blanket of sage and brush. In the brush and the sage, I could see three or four deer and a few antelope. In this scene a buffalo bull was bellowing and screaming. I looked his way and he was pawing the earth, pawing dust upon his back. Above the horizon, I could see an eagle soaring. By that time, the mount of the warrior had spun around. He was eager to run and when the horse spun around, I saw the warrior fully in the face - it was my little brother, Ben.

I called the Swift Hawk family members by phone and told them about this dream. Soon afterwards, we made a hurried trip over there, and I told my sister, Sarah, the dream I had of my little brother. that gave solace and comfort to the family. The dream had quite a few meanings, but in general, it is wonderful and beautiful.

The old Lakota way of life is very precious to me. Relationships were very firm in the Indian world at that time. A common relationship is seen as medicine, as food, and its worth is beyond measure. The relationship entails everything. It entails love, like father-in-law love, mother-in-law love. Love is the main principle in Lakota family life.

Today we hear so much about family child abuse in the newspapers, on the radio, and so on. This type of abuse was unknown in the old Indian world. Relationships and relatives were held in very high esteem. When relatives such as cousins would see each other in the morning, they would shake hands, and then shake hands again if they see each other in the evening. They would go out of their way to do their relations favors. The needs of a relation were considered to be one's own.

An example of the importance of relationships involves two cousins. One cousin was away for quite a while, close to two months. When he returned, he was told that his cousin was very sick. So the first thing he did was saddle his horse to visit his cousin. When he found his cousin in bed, he went to him, shook his hand, and embraced him. There was deep sorrow in the cousin who went to see the sick man, but he did not want to break into crying. He wanted to show his cousin that he was firm and strong. This is the medicine way of the Lakota people.

Today, under the same circumstances, the one going to the sick person might shake the cousin's hand, embrace, and start crying. Crying, in a sense,

SACRED FIREPLACE

weakens a sick person. In the past, everyone knew that. Through the ages, through generations of nature's teachings, people understood that when they see or go to see a sick person, they must be strong. They have one word to give to that one sick person: *blaheceya*. I do not know how to translate that word. But, in the Indian world, they say that is the beginning of a doctoring.

Even when getting a cup of water to give to a sick person, we would say these words: *"Le yatkan yo a nicisni ktalo."* ("Drink this water and you will get well.") Every word, every action in the Lakota world was part of helping one another, reaching out to help. Even common words were said as words of encouragement. These words had strength, gave strength, and also hope.

So, the cousin visited the sick cousin and they talked about old times. Upon leaving his sick relation that evening, he said, "I am going home now, but I will come again tomorrow. But, *tahansi*, get well. We will join the Buffalo Bill Wild West Show in the spring, and we will travel to many cities, maybe cross the ocean together. We will see some sights, so get well. When I get home, I will tell my sisters and my cousins to make you two pairs of beaded moccasins, and two pairs of beaded moccasins for me. I will see to it that I get your Indian regalia completed, and mine also. By the time the Buffalo Bill Wild West Show begins, we should be joined up with the outfit."

This was in the fall. So, through the winter months the sick cousin had his sights set on this Buffalo Bill's Wild West Show, and he worked very hard to get well. And it is told that he did get well,

CEREMONIES

and that both cousins spent six months with the show and then returned home.

SACRED FIREPLACE

Five (Zaptan)

ENDINGS & BEGINNINGS

LAND OF THE WINDS
by *Zintkala Oyate*

The drums beat in rhythmic accord, guttural voices chanted in unison in an ancient tongue. Sorrow is in the surrounding atmosphere; the loss of a precious soul was in the chant that is sung. "The time is right; my life's prayer is done," he had said in the days before his dawn in the journey of eternal life. His last words as dawn broke were, "The answer to my prayer is complete and once

ENDINGS & BEGINNINGS

more is One. I see in the darkest hour before the dawn, the icon of the people, the icon of the Spirit Trail, in the clustering starry heaven's light. There is a new light shining in my soul which encompasses the nature of my being. Great Spirit, Grandfather, with this *Sacred* Pipe I send my spirit, for with my relatives I will live again. Grandfather help me, pity me, I am having a hard time," were his last words as dawn broke.

It is December 3, 1993. At 3:49 in the morning, this holy man, *Petaga Yuha Mani*, was taken back by the Great Spirit (*Wakan Tanka*). This renowned medicine man of the Teton Lakota had been an integral part in bringing the Sundance Ceremony back out into the open. Surely, he shall be missed. There is no confusion among the people of the Lakota *Oyate* who this man was. *Petaga Yuha Mani* was the kind of man who showed the unconquerable force of love and, in so doing, he brought generations together on the plateau of understanding. He had said that, "you cannot force Peace; nor can you buy Peace; only through the love of humanity can we achieve Peace."

Our faith in the dawning motion of creation, with its inspiration of just beliefs, leads us directly to the Sacred Truth—we are all brothers and sisters and that we have a collective inheritance in the love of the Great Spirit. In the heat of misunderstanding, ridicule, and reproach, he took that step in bringing the Pipe religion of the Lakota to the surface for the world to see. He stood forth in developing harmonious relationships with all people.

In September 1990, *Petaga Yuha Mani* traveled to Russia and did a tree planting ceremony with the children. These were his words: "It was cold and windy; I filled my Pipe. I did the ceremony in my own language but, of course, they didn't know the Lakota language. Then, in English, I told the interpreter what I had said... These little children standing here, I want them to go first, to get a handful of dirt and throw it around the tree... He translated what I said to the children and they all moved forward. I continued by telling them that you children gathered here and Russia itself, will grow to see peace and to learn from one another. This tree is young, like you children, and it will grow as you children grow..."

Petaga Yuha Mani was the kind of man who experienced insult and emotional injury yet, he showed and displayed an irrepressible courage with an unshakable faith in his belief in the *Sacred* Pipe. He was a man dedicated to peace and understanding. His vision, his Sacred Dream, brought to him and instilled in him the key. As he would say, "I am in a natural place where the soul constantly expands in the presence of Beauty." As much as he could, he exalted his love of friendships and shared his knowledge wherever and whenever possible. His personal shortcomings did not stop him from hoping to see an illuminated world, filled with love, peace, and true happiness, with the glowing grace of the Great Spirit.

My father's wish was to not be embalmed and to have his body laid to rest east of the *Pte Woku* Sundance area, a distance of perhaps four hundred yards. I recall some of his words at my mother's funeral just three and a half months prior. He had said that, "In the past, the Lakota *Oyate* had their main burial grounds in the sacred Black Hills. There a place had been reserved for chiefs, medicine men, and great warriors, and since the consciousness of America is now more understanding of religious freedom, we should, by all means, establish such a place again."

He said once before that death is not the end, but rather a beginning in the truest form. This, he said, would be the case for men, women, children, and elderly persons who had passed on to the Great Hereafter, the Happy Hunting Grounds, or Heaven. In our language we say, *"Tate Makoca"* which means "Land of the Winds." We understand that we should honor and respect the life of the departed one, that we should acknowledge and accept that individual's principles even though we may not know the extent of them. Last of all, we must obey their final wishes and be happy for them, for they have gone to a place where they have gained the Reality of the Great Spirit, and the magnanimity of Eternity with its Love and Grace.

I recall before my mother's funeral, he came up to me and said that, "We should not cry," and those same words echoed in my mind on the day of his funeral. How could I not cry when I loved him so much? I cannot escape the magnitude of my sorrow. Seeing the many people whom he helped and affected throughout his life, their grieving touched me deeply and I could not take it anymore. I broke down and cried. I could no longer contain my sorrow and so I broke that wish. Yet, in retrospect, I believe that it was meant to be that way. We must understand human nature as our Pipe religion so offers it. We have to experience the quality of our lives in order to fully participate in, understand, and accept life as it is.

SACRED FIREPLACE

On December 7, 1993, the morning of my father's burial, while everything was being prepared, my wife, sisters, brothers, and some close relatives and friends had a small discussion and came to an agreement: that we should have the GiveAway and feeding for the people first. In December, before the equinox, (December 21) when Winter begins, the days are very short. Our concern was with the light of day available to us.

On December 4th and 5th, we had a ground blizzard, also known as a whiteout. The day we brought his body home, the sun was out, it was warm and the sky was blue. The manner in which he had wanted his burial conducted necessitated a one-night wake, with the burial the following afternoon. His casket was sealed and so we had hung his portrait above it. He laid in my mother's house at Mission Flat, a part of the Calico Community, located three miles northwest on Highway 18 from the town of Pine Ridge.

Never to my knowledge had a circumstance such as this ever occurred before. Quite the contrary, usually the departed were buried, then the people were fed, and a GiveAway would occur one year later. As I should have said before, close relatives had donated the cow for beef to make stews and soups for the feed. Other relatives and friends from throughout *Petaga's* life brought flowers, cards, and food in paying him their last respects. A close relative from Manderson was accompanied by a friend who brought his team of horses and wagon for *Petaga Yuha Mani's* last bodily trip.

People came from all across Lakota country, parts of Canada and the United States. In our own

ENDINGS & BEGINNINGS

community where everyone is related, most of us felt that the Great Spirit had let my father live until now. Two years prior, he was given ten days to live and released from the hospital. I was in Florida at the time yet somehow relatives were able to reach me to tell me to return because he was asking for me. I returned home to learn he was staying at one of my sister's friend's homes in the Black Hills. Several of his acquaintances expressed to me, at that time, that he would like to die in the sacred Black Hills.

I thought about that day, more than two years ago, when I was told a Sundance was about to commence west of the town of Custer in the Black Hills. I went to that place and found my father in a square-walled tent. As I entered the tent, there was a soft mattress with bedding and other blankets and quilts. To the immediate left of the entrance, there were many types of food and liquids for him to drink. He was lying on the bed made for him. He looked up and smiled, and that mutual love of father and son that no words can grasp or explain was in the air. I knelt down before him, we embraced, and to this day, I remember my prayer as I had said it then:

"My friends toward the West, You have said, "Look this way. You are the Great Thunder Beings who gather at the setting Sun's horizon. You have made me see.

My friends toward the North, I look that way to see the Buffalo Nation, beautifully coming in a Holy way. You have made me see.

My friend toward the East, my mind transcends there, to see the Elk Nation as They do the Holy

SACRED FIREPLACE

dance in the glorious morning. You have made me see.

My friends toward the South, where the warm winds come, I see the Grey Swan Nation coming this way in their Divine Flight. You have made me see.

My friends toward the Heavens, I see the Holy Swirl of the Spotted Eagle Nation. They have come. They have made me see.

My friends toward the Earth, I feel you, the Medicine Nation, gathering around us. They have made me see.

Wakan Tanka, Skan Skan (the Most Holy), the Sacred Essence moving, let my father live. This year, the summer approaches, I pledge myself to dance the Sundance for all my relatives."

After the GiveAway and feeding the people, we announced that all was in readiness for the funeral procession to begin. The pall bearers, eight in all, assembled along the sides of the casket; they lifted the casket and slowly proceeded to the south door of the house. There, my niece and her husband's pickup truck were waiting nearby. The casket was gently loaded onto the truck bed, and the pall bearers climbed on board and sat on the truck bed sides.

I told this truck to go slow. Following close behind was another pickup truck where there was a drum and Sundance singers from all across Lakota country. They were singing traditional Sundance songs. We went south from my mother's home for three quarters of a mile to the black top Highway 18, and from there we turned right towards the

ENDINGS & BEGINNINGS

Black Hills. Within a mile we approached the Catholic church, with Highway 18 going in between two of its graveyards. We passed the church and went for another mile and a half, and stopped at the turn-off for the road to the *Pte Woku* (Feeding of the Buffalo) Sundance area.

We transferred his body from the pickup truck to the horse-drawn wagon, the buckboard, as some people know it. In spite of the mud, the melting snow, and the growing sadness becoming more and more prominent in all of us in the funeral procession, we still had that sense of kinship which makes the community become strong. Infirmed in dreariness, suffering with the pain of our loss, we remained solemn. I glanced around looking at the people, and in their eyes and through my mind's eye, I could feel their encouragement with its loving affinity. And yes, though we were shrouded in our grieving, we were still One. One people drawn together, as this world will one day be.

We had two miles of mud and melting snow yet to go through, with hills and two places to cross where a creek had once been but which now was a dry creek bed full of snow that had been plowed earlier. The team and wagon continued slowly. Following closely behind was the truck with the Sundance singers. As I heard the echoing melody of the songs in the valley, I seemed to feel his presence, and knowing this I knew that he was approving and happy that this day was just as it should be. Our trek was a slow and winding one. Sometimes the team and wagon had to be pushed by hand by the pall bearers and those who chose to walk behind the wagon which carried *Petaga Yuha Mani* to his grave site.

SACRED FIREPLACE

We stopped a hundred yards from the grave site. From there, the pall bearers and others, who felt reverence, contributed by helping to carry the casket. It was no easy task, going those last hundred yards. It was then that a thought entered my mind. I remembered a time when he and I had visited this place, and as we stood on that grassy little knoll, he spoke of times past. He said that when he first married my mother, he had come through here with everything that he owned at that time. This consisted of a team and wagon plus a saddle horse, and on top of the wagon, there was a plow. Later he used that plow to till a garden for our family and for several others. He said, at that time, that he would rest his body here among the rolling hills and breaks with the large and small pine trees. And there, up above where the dry creek bed is, that is where his last resting place is.

The snow was between ankle and knee deep as we started up the first rise, a small flat area where years before, there had stood a windmill where cattle and horses drank their daily water. This flat area is below the grave site and is perhaps fourteen yards across. We moved slowly and silently. There were a few people already up at the grave site when we started up the steep slope to it.

The grave was set north to south. Toward the West was a green tobacco pouch flag signifying the Thunder Beings. Toward the north was a red tobacco pouch flag signifying the Buffalo Nation. Towards the east was a yellow tobacco pouch flag signifying the Elk Nation. Toward the south was a white tobacco pouch flag signifying the Gray Swan Nation (you can use white or gray). All these flags were set in the ground seven yards from the grave

ENDINGS & BEGINNINGS

itself. On the south side, between the flag and the grave, we had erected a scaffold and placed upon it, in the shape of a man, a bundle into which we had put his personal belongings.

I was standing southeast of the grave between the yellow and white tobacco pouch flags. The casket was brought to a stop between the white and green tobacco pouch flags. It was slowly taken clockwise to the East with its yellow tobacco pouch flags. Then it was brought into the *hocoka* (circle). Within the *hocoka* at the East was a fire which had been tended for some time, and there were some rocks there that had been heated in the fire earlier. The casket was purified by putting water upon the heated stones, while the pall bearers held the casket above the heated rocks and the rising steam. The casket was then taken to the grave, where it was gently set down above the grave pit on four iron bars set in place for it to rest upon.

The Sundance singers began the sacred Pipe Filling Song. The assistant walked to the casket and draped a red cloth over it. I called to a nephew who had given this holy man a beaded case and knife to take with him. I put it on the casket near the bowl of water that was also there. The assistant began to light the twisted sweetgrass braid to smudge the simple altar of the Sundance Nation. By doing this, we envision the reality of *Wohpe* and when we smell its lovely fragrance, our thoughts transcend to Her. The Lakota Oyate know and feel *Wohpe (Buffalo Calf Pipe Woman)* as a Medium - with Her is Beauty beyond compare, and Compassion of the heart. Her Father, *Wakan Tanka*, gave to Her the powers of a Goddess.

SACRED FIREPLACE

As the assistant finished filling it, he motioned to me to receive the *Sacred* Pipe, and I then received it. Next, he motioned to my two sisters to hold a separate white flag, outstretched lengthwise at the South. This white flag signifies the Spirit Trail and, once torn in the middle, the deceased is left to travel the Spirit Trail to the Land of the Winds. My sister, Cynthia, helped her sister tear the cloth, as my brothers Paul and Isaac stood silently upright in agreement, with myself holding the *Sacred* Pipe, ever upward, ever pointing towards the Spirit Trail.

Then I told a nephew, who lives nearby, to ignite the scaffold and I motioned to the Sundance singers for them to start singing the traditional Sundance songs of the Sundance Nation. It was then that I sensed him near the grave, dancing to the beat of the drum. My spirit was filled with silent Majesty, the ecstasy of Joy. I was overwhelmed to know that he was happy, "the finale" true Happiness one can hope to attain, the Love of the Great Spirit.

A MEMORIAL TO
PETE AND AMELIA CATCHES
OCETI WAKAN

b*y* Zintkala Oyate

I write this in the form in which it belongs. The generations who have survived from what has fallen at Wounded Knee 1890 to its present day, have only survived because of the Seven

Sacred Rites bestowed upon the Lakota Nation, perhaps because they are the Sundance Nation.

You will hear, from his own words, the dilemma facing our beleaguered people. **Petaga Yuha Mani,** *as a holy man who loved God, was a simple servant of a Nation in a spiritual depression. With that knowledge, he filled his Sacred Pipe with love for his people. In his heart, he felt the sadness and wanted the world to know that which is in the following texts and how this Vision, this Dream, can and will help ALL peoples.*

The Vision is real, as real as the glorious Sunrise. May Love be the virtue of Life itself, to gain an everlasting, beautiful Enlightenment of God's Eternity.

The Greatest Evil of our Time

The greatest evil of our time is alcohol and drug abuse. Alcohol is causing tears to flow in the Indian country. In the course of six weeks, my wife and I have attended seven wakes and funerals. Most were alcohol-related deaths. Even babies die from alcohol - they do not use it, but they get run over or other things happen to them, and it is sad to see. One baby that died through alcohol-related causes was from my big brother's family line. The next baby that died was from my blind sister's family line. They were little children, they were good children; they were innocent children.

One of the seven funerals was in the Rosebud country. I mentioned earlier that the Rosebud country is where I was adopted into a family in 1968. The family's name is Swift Hawk. I got an emergency call that one of my family members passed away, so my wife, my son, and I went there. That death was alcohol-related. He was a young man in his sixties. He was beaten to death. His head was crushed in. It seems like that is just all I did was to go to funerals. It really saddens my heart. It really shakes me up because of the death of my relations.

I do not like to see people crying. I want to see happiness in people. You see a child laughing and playing, and it does your heart good. That is the way life should be. I had to go to all the wakes and funerals because the deceased are a part of our people. I know them. We shed tears nearly every day because of these things that trouble our people, that cause orphans, that cause loved ones to go away into the next world.

I do not know if there is a power so great that it could lessen this problem that we are facing now. We have a tribal council, a legislative body to oversee the tribe. Whatever the welfare of the tribe is, whatever the problems the tribe has, I doubt if there is a councilman big enough to attack this problem of alcohol.

At another reservation, the Tribal Council went to war against alcohol recently. There you have a bunch of people fighting a war against alcohol. It was good, oh so good, when I heard this on the radio. I admire the people that initiated this. The whole Council went and stepped behind and supported it. Not only the Council supported this but those that work in public places, like the Tribal

Law and Order Committee, the policemen, the judges, and whatever personnel involved in working for the Tribe. If they are convicted on an alcohol-related charge, even drunken driving, they are given a chance to rehabilitate by going to treatment voluntarily. They can come back to their jobs when they finish their treatment. But if they do not go to treatment, then it is goodbye for them. They are going to be left out.

I think I like this. It takes a heck of a lot of leadership. That kind of leadership is what the Pine Ridge Indian Reservation needs. It is the kind of leadership that you see in the DADD organization, Dads Against Drunk Driving. They are walking the highway in protest of the things that are going wrong here. I admire them. I work with them. They too, are my relatives. Another organization is MADD, Mothers Against Drunk Driving and another is SADD, Students Against Drunk Driving. This is needed very much. We made the public aware of these organizations. The protests and marches we did went through the air, through KILI radio station. It went through the Lakota Times, it went through the Rapid City Journal. Now these organizations are known throughout the United States. The Lakota Times paper reaches overseas, in Canada, and other places.

I hope and pray that our Tribal Council on the Pine Ridge Reservation passes a resolution like the other reservation did and supports it 100%, because that is the guiding way. They are the leaders. They are supposed to live as role models for the people to follow. Law officers, in the same light, should be working as role models.

SACRED FIREPLACE

The Oglala Sioux Tribal Council on several occasions, wanted to legalize alcohol. The issue went to a referendum, and the people did not want it. A lot more could be said. A lot more, with tears, with all the sadness. That is as much as I want to say about alcohol and the Tribal Council.

But let me say this: It does not matter who it is, or what profession a person has, what career a person has, if he has a bottle of alcohol, whether it is beer, wine, or whatever, in one hand. I do not look at him as a man. In order to do good, dependable work, a man must do away with that bottle and live in Sobriety for people to see. He does not have to advertise. He can live like that and people will notice. This is where trust begins, and this is where trust will remain. This is how we will love one another. This is how Sobriety is so good.

Sobriety is hard to live by when all the world around you is a drinking people. But Sobriety to me is the one thing that the so-called Jesus Christ would love to see and would like to embrace a person, man or woman, for being in Sobriety. *Tunkasila, Wakan Tanka*, loves a person that does not use alcohol. Because, as I said, alcohol is the ruin of our people. It is putting people into the ground. Alcohol would not be in our world if we had strong leaders like Crazy Horse and Sitting Bull. These men were true leaders and they loved their people. They looked only to the good that their people may have, and in that way, they wanted their people to live. There is no one like them now.

When the white man came west, he brought the evil with him. He brought his rot-gut whiskey, syphilis, gonorrhea, and now AIDS. If we were left

ENDINGS & BEGINNINGS

alone as we had lived before the advance of the white man, we would still be able to live good, take care of our welfare, teach our children respectability, to respect the elders, the sick, to help one another, to live in harmony, to live clean and good. This is how *Wakan Tanka* made us.

That was the way we knew this world to be. Everything was pure. The streams ran pure and good. The mind and the heart of every Indian was pure and good and clean. Ever since the white man came west, he brought all the evil along with him. We should live good. We should be happy. But, can we be happy with all the tears? Can we be happy with all this alcohol and drugs around us? Even though a person may die a natural death, he is bothered in his lifetime with alcohol. Even though he does not drink at all, his friends, his relatives bother him for money. They want to borrow money or hock stuff, you name it. They knock at your door at all hours of the night and day. They stop you in the street and ask you for a quarter. Sometimes I go without because I do not have it. Sometimes my car runs near empty, and here, one guy reaches out, asks for a quarter.

We realize alcohol will remain with us. But our hope, our prayer, is to get drunk drivers off the road because, through drunk driving, there is a lot of misery, a lot of pain and suffering. Some people are crippled for life. Some meet their life's end there and it is sad.

I hear many people saying we are having these problems because some do not do the Sundance right, they do not do the sweat lodge right, and they do not do the Pipefast right, and suffering falls upon

SACRED FIREPLACE

the people. In the many Sundances throughout the Reservation, I see dancers that partake of food and water in the evening, and that is all wrong. We should try to do at least a portion of the Sundance the authentic way, the way it was originally done.

Our forefathers have done the real Sundance, they have done the real Pipefast, and they have done the real sweat lodge ceremony. So, why could not we continue with the tradition that was sacred to our people, that was sacred to *Wakan Tanka*? I know He loves us. Why did He give us these seven sacred rites? In doing these ceremonies in the way, the traditional way, that He gave them to us, we can communicate with Him, and He can do for us what we ask.

I used to drink. I used to be a drunkard. I used to go to jail. But I quit, all on my own. I quit not because I was sick of it with cirrhosis. I quit not because I went to AA (Alcoholics Anonymous) meetings or to treatment. I quit sort of on my own. Not really on my own but *Wakan Tanka* loved me. So, in turn, I pledged that all the remaining portion of my life will be in Sobriety. That is a hard commitment to make.

I used to listen to people who said, "I am going to quit for forty days." These are people who go to church. Through Lent they abstain from some things that they like. Some abstain from smoking, some from alcohol, some say they are going to cut down on their food consumption.

The way I quit was when, one day, I got up with a hangover. I had a very splitting headache. Out of habit, I began looking for some beer. I would usually find it outside somewhere because I had been sitting outside and drinking and leaving some there. Or I would look in the refrigerator over in the next house. I went through the whole bit and could not find anything. So, I came back and sat on my bed. At the head of my bed was an apple box. On the box stood a lamp and "the makings," as we call it—Bull Durham, cigarette paper, and matches. And sitting there thinking about it, I looked up and there, in plain sight on the table, stood a whole pint of wine. Not even the seal was broken.

I had mixed feelings. I was glad but yet, when I looked at that wine, a thought came to me. I thought of *Wakan Tanka*, why he made me and a thought came to me: If I lived in that old Indian world, I would have been a warrior. Most certainly, I would have been a warrior, and a warrior fights enemies. So looking at that wine, I said, "*Wakan Tanka* make me a warrior." I got up and went over to that bottle of wine, I hit the bottle three or four times, broke the seal, and unscrewed the cap. And I said this, "*Wakan Tanka* made me a warrior and you are the enemy of the people. This moment you and I clash in a struggle, in a fight—I, as a warrior, you, as an enemy of me and the Lakota people." I opened the door, stepped outside on the porch, and I turned that bottle upside down.

There was an inner thought inside of me, "Turn it back over, save a mouthful," that sort of thing. It was the other part that was no good in me that was saying this. But I held on to that statement, saying, "I am a warrior and we are in a struggle." I emptied the whole bottle, and I held it in my hand. I said out loud, "Today I conquered you and I scalped you." Then I threw that bottle as far as I could and I said, "A warrior is honored by the scalps that he

SACRED FIREPLACE

acquires. But I do not even want your scalp. I will throw that away, too." Then I threw the cap away. And to this day, I have not drank a drop of any kind of alcohol beverage.

So, these are examples of what life is about in our present day. Alcoholism is that way. When we partake of alcohol, we live in sort of an imitation happiness. We do not think right. Everything that we do is false. The happiness we seem to enjoy is false. The laughter is there, but it is false. That is not the real world. The real world is Sobriety. It is a hard world with its many problems. But being sober and honest, living good, that is the real life. This is the life that *Wakan Tanka* loves. This is the life that He wants us to live.

On the other hand, through alcohol and drugs, we cry deep inside for the things alcohol has done to our people. When parents drink, it makes children nervous, causes children to miss school, makes children lose sleep. Sometimes they go to school without having breakfast. Alcohol does that. It takes a cut-across and avoids the real good things. It takes food out of the mouth of children, because parents spend food money on alcohol. This is why I say that *alcohol is the greatest evil of our time*. I wonder how many people think of it this way.

I wonder, too, whether this philosophy I have, believing in the concepts that *Wakan Tanka* gave us - the gifts of the sweat lodge, the Sundance, the Pipefast; even those three, any one of them or all of them, and through them and using the Pipe and its ways, we can meet head on and conquer any problem which may come to us.

ENDINGS & BEGINNINGS

This is why, years ago, I had in my mind to establish this spiritual encampment *Oceti Wakan*. At *Oceti Wakan*, we will do our teaching in our Lakota language, using the Pipe and the Sacred Ceremonies that were given to us by the Great Spirit to overcome the greatest evil of our time, alcohol and drugs. And not only those but the other problems as well.

I am thinking I will say a special prayer for those that use alcohol and drugs because that is not the way to live. I do not care what kind of a job a person may have, if, in one hand, he carries alcohol or drugs, he does not do a good job. He may lose his job, he may lose his family, and he may even lose his life or cause the loss of other people's lives on the highway.

I will ask a special prayer for those of you that may be using alcohol and drugs, to return to the Red Road of Life. In a pleasing way so that the Sunlight, the Blessing of those that have gone before you and are in the Great Hereafter will bless you. I am thinking of all of them. And in that way, I will ask the Great Spirit to bless you, to live as one family, to know each other and understand each other, to communicate with one another, love one another.

I will ask the Great Spirit to bless each and every one of you. And I hope that, through these talks, you will receive some Light to strengthen your faith, to strengthen your trust in the Great Spirit, to live a life that is meant to be good, that is pleasing to the Great Spirit.

They say Forgiveness is a real act of Mercy. If you forgive someone for any wrong that is done to

SACRED FIREPLACE

you, it is the greatest act of Mercy you can render in this life. I ask *Tunkasila*, *Wakan Tanka*, to Bless you all.

PURPOSE OF OCETI WAKAN

As a medicine man, I want to be instrumental in doing things with the *Sacred* Pipe, imploring the

ENDINGS & BEGINNINGS

Great Spirit for the things that mankind cannot do. In trying to explain *Oceti Wakan*, I will say it this way. When the Great Spirit, *Wakan Tanka*, created the world and the many things that comprise this creation, He made people in the many colors that He liked. *Wakan Tanka* likes color. He made the black people, the white people, the yellow people, and the red people. The red people are the Eskimos, the Canadian Indians, the Native Americans of the fifty states and down through Mexico and South America.

To each of these different peoples, He gave a way of life, a culture, a language, heritage, and tradition, each different than the other, because His love is there. To these many different colored peoples that He made, He gave to each a way to worship. He gave the white people Jesus Christ; to others, He gave Buddha, to others a different one. He gave the Lakota people a way of life, a language to pray to Him, a culture completely different from that of the others. It is through this system of prayer and language, a way of life, that we can address any of the problems that may assail us in this life on earth.

To the Lakota people, He gave the *Sacred* Pipe to pray with. The Lakota people, I believe most sincerely, can stop this alcohol and drug abuse through the use of the *Sacred* Pipe in the proper way, and through the language, the culture, the traditions, as they were given to us many centuries before the white men arrived on these shores. This will bring us back to ourselves as we were created. This will heal the shame that was given to us as children when we had no wisdom, as we were told we were lesser because we were Lakota and spoke

SACRED FIREPLACE

only Lakota. That deep shame that has brought so much destruction to us needs to be healed, as it was a lie.

Oceti Wakan will be unique. It will be a place of Worship. One of the four things that Lakota people use in praying to the Great Spirit is fire. As I have said, *Oceti Wakan* means Sacred Fireplace, it is one of the places we pray from. A sacred fireplace denotes the fire pit at the head of the sweat lodge, and the sacred fireplace is where the fire is built during a Sundance. The sweat lodge will be conducted year round. I am old now, and I cannot go to a sweat lodge in the winter time when it is cold. But, the winter sweat lodge will be built inside a ceremonial house with a dirt floor and the summer sweat lodge will be out in the open. And if it should rain during the summertime, we can go in that house and still conduct our sweat lodge. Maybe we will have a Sweat Lodge Ceremony every morning or every evening. This is what we call Indian Time. It does not have to be one particular time. I remember one day, we had several Sweat Lodge Ceremonies. We had two before noon, one at daybreak, one about ten o'clock. Then one about two or two-thirty and one before the sun set. We had four Sweat Lodge Ceremonies in one day. *Oceti Wakan* would be something like this. It would be a cleansing place. The Sweat Lodge Ceremony is really a cleansing, a purifying ceremony. It cleanses the spirit and it cleanses the body, the physical being.

ENDINGS & BEGINNINGS

SOUTH INTERIOR PERSPECTIVE

Model/Interior of Ceremonial/Education Center for Oceti Wakan[10]

---

[10] Kathleen Chesley of Frank Lloyd Wright Architecture School did the architectural drawings and built this model of Oceti Wakan. She lovingly donated her time because she said the sweat lodge changed her life.

SACRED FIREPLACE

Life is real. We are in this life just once and the days we live pass on by. They will never come back again. So, from this aspect, from this vision, I know *Oceti Wakan*, if it can ever develop the funds to build it, will do good for the people. I have not much more in life to go. So, while I am able, I wish to put everything that I can into it. My heart is in it; my mind is in it, my body is in it, my spirit is in it. And if it is the will of the Great Spirit, it shall come to pass. If it does not ever get off the ground, then I know it is not the time. Then I would know that the Great Spirit has a time for such an endeavor and maybe, with somebody more worthy than I am. If I am unworthy, I will know that this thing will not come to pass. My son will work to make it a reality.

This is the way I want to teach. This is the way I want to instill in their minds and hearts the faith so strong that, without medicine, but with the faith and trust in the Great Spirit, they can be cured of any terrible disease such as alcohol and drugs. With this faith and trust in the Great Spirit, anyone can be cured, because that is His word. And if we live in that way, we will know we are part of His creation, that we are part of this growing Earth. From a sad state of alcoholism, we can become whole again, become rich in spirit, become loved by the Great Spirit because we are a part of His creation.

My philosophy is this: There is, in this creation, *Wakan Tanka*, and He created man. He instilled into every human being a Source of Power, a Gift, and with that, he can overcome any amount of problems in his whole lifespan. But a lot of people do not use this gift to overcome and let that gift lay

ENDINGS & BEGINNINGS

dormant, unused. If we only reach out and look for that Source, that extra strength, we can overcome anything. If we can overcome one problem, we can overcome any other problem which may assail us. That way, we will prove to ourselves and to our God, our *Wakan Tanka*, that His work on Earth, that ,His Creation is growing in His good way in His love.

There are beautiful hills at *Pte Woko*. There are beautiful pines. There are deep canyons; they are all beautiful. God's Hand is there. I want to put my hand next to His and implore Him through these sacred rites, in my own language, to cure our people from the diseases of alcohol and drugs, and live a life that comes from Him, a life in the Light of Truth, in the Light of Love, the beauty of being alive and being good. This is just the beginning of *Oceti Wakan*.

SACRED FIREPLACE

The area of *Oceti Wakan*

EPILOGUE
by Zintkala Oyate

All of us being human and raised the way we are, we cannot truly decide for ourselves who we want to be. Therefore, by the nature of our birth, we cannot choose our color or our place in this society. We cannot change the fact that each and every one of us is unique and that we belong, that there is a place for us in this Sundance Nation.

I will not live under the shadow of the Sacred Tree. Rather, I will glean from its Essence; I will let my soul sparkle in its Light and receive the wisdom from the All Conceiving. For God's own love rustles through the leaves of the sacred Tree of Life in His Spiritual Realm, incomprehensible to our world of light and shadow.

For some, however, it is easy to accept the concept of our Sacred Hoop being broken, easy to accept we are individuals who must "assimilate."

Yes, it is easy to accept these matters, yet this does not happen to me. I cannot, and will not, accept a way that is not virtuous. All that I can do is look at it and feel the depression and despair gnawing at me. The only thing that overshadows this spiritual depression is the realization that I am a human being with all the liveliness to live in harmony. The Great Spirit has put me here to live as a part of His creation, to respect the Mother Earth, the Sky, the Sun, all creatures and, yes, the great wonder of each Direction.

Lakota people and other Native peoples in their communities who know of the four Virtues of the Man and Woman and, who choose to live virtuously, are not wrong. We choose to live this way religiously. *This means that the genuinely unspeakable horror of some matters in our lives is not enough of an excuse for refusing to face them.* The problem that we face today in dealing with Institutional Racism is that it has become an integral part of the very fabric of Thought itself, and thus supports and moves our Society without people being aware of it, to some degree.

We are under programs that are supposedly working towards the elimination of Institutional Racism. But it seems that there are those who really do not want this to happen. Instead of being used to eliminate prejudice, the information collected by these programs is used, instead, to further feed the horrible spirit of Racism. The injustice caused by this hideous idea in Society has affected us, everyone, and I truly believe that it is causing this spiritual depression in modern day living. *It has prevented us from grasping the true nature of the classification of human beings.*

SACRED FIREPLACE

As for myself, a Lakota living on the Pine Ridge Indian Reservation in South Dakota, I do feel depressed looking at our society. Although I am condemned to live in poverty yet, I hold close in my heart, the determination of the original Common Man, to remain as I am, affirming the traditional and rejecting the "modern" on ethical grounds. We, as a people, know of the Presence and Love of the Great Spirit, and the vital importance of the people coming together, and of following the Virtues and living in the traditional manner. Choosing to live virtuously is good for the Lakota, and, as my father said many times, we must live that way in our home, in our community, and in the Nation. As it was in the past, so is it now in the present and will continue to be in the coming tomorrow; a Lakota needs to be reminded and reassured of this to possess common self-respect.

Now let me wander back to when I was a boy. When I was a young boy, I was seeking a spiritualism that, perhaps, comes from the Dawn of Time. Although there are many forms of it, we have to choose for ourselves which path to follow. There are many churches, religions, and denominations, all crying the word of God. This makes the logical mind hesitate. First, you must realize that *God is the Great Mystery* that cannot be classified, nor can ever be understood by man. Second, you must realize that people are suffering from a disease that is self-inflicted and that, perhaps, this infliction is a degeneration of the spirit that is caused by doctrines of man. I know that, as a child growing up on the reservation, I had an inferiority complex which led me to believe that I had no right to pray, that my father (whom I loved so much) was a

ENDINGS & BEGINNINGS

medicine man the other children at school called a witch doctor and a disciple of the devil, even though my father healed people who were turned away from the hospital because they were considered hopeless.

I remember beautiful days with laughter, caring and harmony inside the family as I grew. That changed with the beginning of my education. I came to think of myself first and others last. I learned to be crafty and to disguise my feelings for my benefit. I did not know *that these were the first symptoms of the degeneration of the spirit.* I would go to church with no feeling, just going through the motions, so to speak. Yet, when I went to a Pipe Ceremony, I was completely different. I became ebullient and satisfied from its beginning to its conclusion.

The realization that I belonged in this experiential religion came as a shock to me. Though I denied it at first, because of the years of brainwashing, I knew that, within me, was an empathy of the spirit that belonged. I then began to help my father at the Sundance. I must warn you that not everyone can do this. For it is a gift from the Great Spirit that a man is chosen and is able to run this Festival of Light, where man and all Creation become One. The Sundance, under the direction of the mediator, is propelled within the very nest of Creation itself. It is a time when one's spirit is openly seen, heard, felt, smelled, and touched by an equality of all of the living. Although the Sundance is misunderstood by outsiders, its essence is the Hoop of the World, where all the world becomes one Community.

SACRED FIREPLACE

At *Oceti Wakan* we will confront these issues of spiritual depression in ourselves and mend those inconsistencies in our path towards a wholeness. We will look from modern windows and re-awaken that deep traditional voice. We will hear its expressions, and feel its impressions in the vastness of our souls, and become complete again.

Living in a world full of prejudices, *we have to look inward to find the true nature of ourselves.* Now is the time to change into enlightenment, to extinguish our old fears of one another, and we will do it together—a prism of Universal Unity.

When this beacon of loving light burns bright in our once dark and lonely domain, we will beat the drums of Unity and shout its songs. For here in America, this young nation of Diversity is destined to attain the complete Love of the Great Mystery. I thank you and may the Great *Wakan Tanka* Bless the steps of your path.

GLOSSARY

Petaga Yuha Mani holding the *Sacred* Pipe
and Eagle Fan, praying to the Great Mystery

SACRED FIREPLACE

GLOSSARY OF LAKOTA WORDS

agito—enlightenment

akisa—to bring blessing on you, many call war cry

Anpetu kile wakan yelo—This is a holy day. T*okahe taku wa yelo*—I am the first relative of this day. *Wanble gleska wan le ya*—A spotted eagle is saying this. *Kinyan u welo*—Flying as he comes. *Anukan san wan le ya*—A bald eagle is saying this.

aka napceunka—nineteen (19)

aka nunpa—twelve (12)

aka sakowin—seventeen (17)

aka sakpe—sixteen (16)

aka topa—fourteen (14)

aka wanji—eleven (11)

aka yamni—thirteen (13)

aka zaptan—fifteen (15)

blaheceya—"the beginning of healing"

Brule—Band of the Tetons

Canku Luta—the Red Road

Canupa—*Sacred* Pipe

GLOSSARY

Canupa tawooglake—refers to the Pipe Way, in that whosoever respects, loves, honors, and takes care of the Pipe, will have a long life

cansasa—Indian tobacco, or red willow bark (inside) plus medicine

chatkuta ukea—from the back it comes

ehake eyokpaza—the last dark portion of the night before the first light of dawn

eyokipisni—not happy

Hanbleceya—Pipefast

heyoka—a person who literally does things backwards in a humerous manner but whose spirit helpers are the powerful Thunder Beings

hocoka—circle of prayer ceremony

hokahey—a message of movement, command

Hunkapi—Making of a relative

Hunkpapa—village at the end, Band of Tetons

igmu ska wan he—white cat came

Inipi—Purification Rite

initi—purification structure

kakala—grandfather

Ka Sapa—Black Hills

kinyan u welo—flying as he comes

Lakota—the first people of peace

Le miyaca nawajin yelo—This is I that is standing.

Wa mung yanka—Look at me.

SACRED FIREPLACE

Lena ota makuye—I want more like this

Le yatkan yo a nicisni ktalo—Drink this water and you will get well

maka mani ukea—close and on the ground it comes

Mitakuye Oyasin—All My Relations

naca—leader

nagi—your spirit, soul

napceunka—nine (9)

nunpa—two (2)

Oceti Wakan—Sacred Fireplace

Okawinga Win—Perpetual Cycle Woman

Oglala—scattered, Band of the Tetons

Owanka Nasto—song during which everyone present dances around the Sundance Tree that has just been planted

oyate—people, community, nation

Pahan San Oyate—Gray Swan Nation

peji—marijuana, grass

pow wow—originally know as *Osmaha Wacipa*, but now is contest based

Pte Woku—Feeding of the Buffalo

saglogan—eight (8)

sakowin—seven (7)

sakpe—six (6)

sihanskala—long feet

GLOSSARY

spaniciya—burnt himself

tahansi—cousin

Taku Skan Skan—Most Holy Judge, Sacred Essence Moving

taniga—tripe (cow)

Tatanka Oyate—Buffalo Nation

Tate Makoca—Land of the Winds, Heaven

tiyospaye—community

teepee—home

Tetons—*Hunkpapa* (Camp at the Horn End), *Sicunga* (Burnt Thigh), *Minneconjou* (Use Water in Planting), *Oglala* (Scattered), *Sihasapa* (Blackfeet), *Oohenunpa* (Two Kettle), and *Itazipco* (No Bow)

Tokala—Kit Fox Society, the work force

topa—four (4)

tunkan—the birth and the aged (the grandfathers) once inside the Purification Rite

Tunkasila—Grandfathers (spirit world)

Tunkasila, Wakan Tanka, onsimilaye ikce wicasa unsiya makakija. Mi takuye kakijapi wakin ya ikca wicasa ta cannunpa wan yuha. Hoye ciciye.—Grandfather, Great Mystery, have pity on me. As a common man I am having a hard time. I carry the burden of my relatives with the common man's *Sacred* Pipe, I implore you.

Tunkasila wa mung yanka yo—Grandfathers, look at me

tunska—nephew

SACRED FIREPLACE

unci—grandmother

Wakan Tanka—Great Mystery, Great Spirit, The Most Holy, God

wakanyeja—sacred being, child

Wakinyan—Thunder Beings

wakunka—elderly

Wanble Gleska—The Spotted Eagle

wanji—one (1)

wasa—red paint made from clay and fat

wasicu—white man; originally "fat takers"

wasna—dried meat, ground with choke cherries

wateca—portion of food taken home from a feast

Wohpe—Daughter of *Taku Skan Skan*. *Pte San Win* (Grey Calf Pipe Woman) from antiquity; brought the *Lakotas* the Seven Sacred Rites

wicemna—ten (10)

Wiscasa wan kaiglaglag—the radiantly Golden Man

Wiwangyang Wacipi—the Sundance; gazing at the sun they dance

wojapi—berry pudding

yamni—three (3)

yuwipi—tied

zaptan—five (5)